rice
& *risotto*

rice
& risotto

GREAT WAYS WITH A CLASSIC INGREDIENT

Consultant Editor: **ROZ DENNY**

LORENZ BOOKS

Published in 1999 by Lorenz Books

© Anness Publishing Limited 1996, 1999, 2000

Lorenz Books is an imprint of
Anness Publishing Limited
Hermes House
88-89 Blackfriars Road
London SE1 8HA

This edition distributed in Canada by Raincoast Books
8680 Cambie Street, Vancouver, British Columbia V6P 6M9

ISBN 0-7548-0303-1

A CIP catalogue record for this book is available from the British Library

Publisher: Joanna Lorenz
Senior Cookery Editor: Linda Fraser
In-house Editor: Anne Hildyard
Designer: Ian Sandom
Cover Design: Balley Design Associates
Photography: Karl Adamson, Edward Allwright, David Armstrong,
Steve Baxter, James Duncan, Patrick McLeavey, Amanda Heywood,
and Michael Michaels
Styling: Madeleine Brehaut, Maria Kelly, Blake Minton, and Kirsty Rawlings
Food for Photography: Carla Capalbo, Elizabeth Wolf-Cohen, Joanna Craig,
Carole Handslip, Jane Hartshorn, Wendy Lee, Annie Nichols, Jane Stevenson,
and Steven Wheeler
Special Photography: Janine Hosegood
Illustrator: Madeleine David

Front cover: William Lingwood, Photographer; Helen Trent, Stylist;
Sunil Vijayakar, Home Economist

Previously published as part of the *Creative Cooking Library*

Printed and bound in Hong Kong/China

1 3 5 7 9 10 8 6 4 2

NOTES

For all recipes, quantities are given in both metric and imperial measures and,
where appropriate, measures are also given in standard cups and spoons.
Follow one set, but not a mixture because they are not interchangeable.

Standard spoon and cup measurements are level.
1 tbsp = 15ml, 1 tsp = 5ml, 1 cup = 250ml/8fl oz

Australian standard tablespoons are 20ml. Australian readers should use 3 tsp
in place of 1 tbsp for measuring small quantities of gelatine, cornflour, salt etc.

Medium eggs should be used unless otherwise stated.

CONTENTS

INTRODUCTION

Around two-thirds of the world's population is nourished every day on rice. There are thought to be about 7,000 varieties of rice grown across the globe, all with different qualities and characteristics. Rice is central to many of the world's greatest cuisines and can be used in a host of ways both savoury and sweet. No other food is quite this versatile. In the West, we have just begun to appreciate the great potential of this glorious grain. Instead of relegating it to the side of our plates as an accompaniment used to mop up a little sauce or pad out the appearance of a plate, we now look on rice as the basis of a delicious meal.

The term "rice" should be applied to the milled grain only. The actual plant is known as paddy. Rice grains come from an aquatic plant that requires a great deal of water during its early growth. It was one of the first cereals to be cultivated thousands of years ago from a variety of wild grasses in many different parts of Asia. There was no one specific birthplace. The numerous varieties common today in rice-eating countries evolved according to the climate and terrain and the developing agricultural practices of the time. Even today, new strains are being developed or discovered – the latest is red rice from the Camargue in France. Rice is a very adaptable plant. Some varieties need a lot of water for growth, others can survive on less. There are grains that need constant warmth, whilst others can tolerate cold spells, which is why rice can be easily cultivated in so many parts of the world.

Broadly speaking, there are two main "groups" of rice which are categorized botanically into either long grain (*Oryza indica*) or short grain (*Oryza japonica*) and this determines whether the rices are long and separate, chubby and creamy or stubby and sticky. *Indica* rices have higher levels of amylose starch which keeps them more separate after cooking. *Japonica* rices (commonly known as short or round grain rices) are higher in amylopectin which gives them a more starchy quality. Needless to say, some rices fall between these two main categories, displaying aspects of both, such as Thai fragrant rices that are long grain and lightly sticky. Plentiful supplies of water are important at the early growth of both types of grains. In the early dawn of civilisation, this led to the need for irrigation. Controlling water supplies required great social organisation if every field of paddy were to get the right amount of water. Strong social structures began to develop in rice areas, which in turn had a great effect on the cultural origins of many rice-eating civilisations. Small wonder then that rice began to play a great part in the religion and myths of these areas – unlike any other food. Legends, stories and ceremonies developed around rice. Gods and goddesses had to be humoured with gifts of rice. The grains came to symbolize fertility. No other food in the world is held in such esteem or represents the soul of a people the way rice does in many parts of Asia.

This respect for rice continues on into each Asian home where rice is central to daily cooking, and great skill and techniques are handed down through generations of cooks. The very smell of rice cooking is the sign of a warm welcome for visitors to a home and even everyday greetings include references to the eating of rice.

The main rice-growing regions of the world are China, Japan, India, Indonesia, Thailand, the southern states of the USA and areas of Spain and Italy. However, many of these countries consume their own rices, so little finds its way to the West. Thailand is known as the great rice bowl of Asia as it

Women harvesting the rice crop on the Indonesian island of Bali.

MID-WEEK MEALS

Rice is the ideal store cupboard food. As long as it is kept clean and dry it will keep indefinitely and is ready to be cooked at a moment's notice. Tipped straight from the pack when a main meal is on order but time is short, rice will form the basis of a satisfying, tasty dish easy to eat either at the table or from a tray. Risottos, pilaffs and stir-fries are natural partners with simple fresh foods such as bacon, prawns, flaked fish, chicken and minced meats. Serve any of these dishes with a crisp salad or lightly boiled green vegetables.

Fish with Rice

This Arabic fish dish, *Sayadich* is especially popular in Lebanon.

INGREDIENTS

Serves 4–6
juice of 1 lemon
45ml/3 tbsp oil
900g/2lb cod steaks
4 large onions, chopped
5ml/1 tsp ground cumin
2–3 saffron strands
1 litre/1³/₄ pints/4 cups fish stock
450g/1lb/generous 2¹/₄ cups basmati or
   long grain rice
50g/2oz/¹/₄ cup pine nuts,
   lightly toasted
salt and ground black pepper
fresh parsley, to garnish

1 Blend the lemon juice and 15ml/1 tbsp of oil in a shallow dish. Add the fish, turn to coat thoroughly, then cover and marinate for 30 minutes.

2 Heat the remaining oil in a large saucepan and fry the onions for 5–6 minutes, stirring occasionally.

3 Drain the fish, reserving the marinade, and add to the pan. Fry for 1–2 minutes each side until lightly golden, then add the cumin, saffron strands and a little salt and pepper.

4 Pour in the fish stock and the reserved marinade, bring to the boil and then simmer for 5–10 minutes or until the fish is nearly done.

5 Transfer the fish to a plate and add the rice to the stock. Bring to the boil, reduce the heat and simmer gently for 15 minutes until nearly all the stock has been absorbed.

6 Arrange the fish on top of the rice and cover the pan. Steam over a low heat for 15–20 minutes.

7 Transfer the fish to a plate, then spoon the rice onto a large flat dish and arrange the fish on top. Sprinkle with toasted pine nuts and garnish with fresh parsley.

Rice Layered with Prawns

INGREDIENTS

Serves 4–6
2 large onions, sliced and deep fried
300ml/¹/₂ pint/1¹/₄ cups natural yogurt
30ml/2 tbsp tomato purée
60ml/4 tbsp green masala paste
30ml/2 tbsp lemon juice
salt, to taste
5ml/1 tsp black cumin seeds
5cm/2in cinnamon stick
4 green cardamom pods
450g/1lb fresh king prawns, peeled
   and de-veined
225g/8oz/3 cups button mushrooms
225g/8oz/2 cups frozen peas, thawed
450g/1lb/generous 2¹/₄ cups basmati
   rice soaked for 5 minutes in boiled
   water and drained
300ml/¹/₂ pint/1¹/₄ cups water
1 sachet saffron powder mixed in
   90ml/6 tbsp milk
30ml/2 tbsp ghee or unsalted butter

1 Mix the first 9 ingredients together in a large bowl. Mix the prawns, mushrooms and peas into the marinade and leave for about 2 hours.

2 Grease the base of a heavy pan and add the prawns, vegetables and any marinade juices. Cover with the drained rice and smooth the surface gently until you have an even layer.

3 Pour the water all over the surface of the rice. Make random holes through the rice with the handle of a spoon and pour in the saffron milk.

4 Place a few knobs of ghee or butter on the surface and place a circular piece of foil directly on top of the rice. Cover and steam over a low heat for 45–50 minutes, until the rice is cooked Gently toss the rice, prawns and vegetables together and serve hot.

Pumpkin and Pistachio Risotto

This elegant combination of creamy golden rice and orange pumpkin can be made as pale or as bright as you like by adding different quantities of saffron.

INGREDIENTS

Serves 4

1.2 litres/2 pints/5 cups vegetable stock
   or water
generous pinch of saffron strands
30ml/2 tbsp olive oil
1 onion, chopped
2 garlic cloves, crushed
900g/2lb/7 cups pumpkin, peeled,
   seeded and cut into 2cm/³/₄in cubes
450g/1lb/generous 2¼ cups risotto rice
200ml/7fl oz/scant 1 cup dry
   white wine
30ml/2 tbsp Parmesan cheese,
   finely grated
50g/2oz/¼ cup pistachios
45ml/3 tbsp chopped fresh marjoram
   or oregano, plus leaves to garnish
salt, freshly grated nutmeg and ground
   black pepper

1 Bring the stock or water to the boil and reduce to a low simmer. Ladle a little of it into a small bowl. Add the saffron strands and leave to infuse.

2 Heat the oil in a large saucepan. Add the onion and garlic and cook gently for about 5 minutes until softened. Add the pumpkin and rice and cook for a few more minutes until the rice looks transparent.

3 Pour in the wine and allow it to bubble hard. When it is absorbed add a quarter of the hot stock or water and the infused saffron liquid. Stir until all the liquid has been absorbed.

4 Gradually add the stock or water, a ladleful at a time, allowing the rice to absorb the liquid before adding more, and stirring all the time. After 20–30 minutes the rice should be golden yellow, creamy and *al dente*.

5 Stir in the Parmesan cheese, cover the pan and leave the risotto to stand for 5 minutes.

6 To finish, stir in the pistachios and marjoram or oregano. Season to taste with a little salt, nutmeg and pepper, and scatter over a few marjoram or oregano leaves.

Bacon Risotto

Smoky bacon and mushrooms add an earthy flavour to this simple risotto.

INGREDIENTS

Serves 4

30ml/2 tbsp sunflower oil
1 large onion, chopped
75g/3oz/½ cup smoked
  bacon, chopped
350g/12oz/scant 1½ cups risotto rice
1–2 garlic cloves, crushed
15g/½ oz/¼ cup dried sliced
  mushrooms, soaked in boiling water
175g/6oz/generous 2 cups mixed
  fresh mushrooms
1.2 litres/2 pints/5 cups hot stock
few sprigs of oregano or thyme
15g/½ oz/1 tbsp butter
a little dry white wine
45ml/3 tbsp chopped, peeled tomatoes
8–10 black olives, stoned and quartered
salt and ground black pepper

1 Heat the oil in a large, heavy-based pan with a lid. Gently cook the onion and bacon until the onion is tender and the bacon fat has run out.

2 Stir in the rice and garlic and cook over a high heat for 2–3 minutes, until the rice is well coated.

3 Add the dried mushrooms and their liquid, the fresh mushrooms, half the stock, the oregano or thyme and seasoning. Bring gently to the boil, then reduce the heat to low. Cover tightly and leave to cool.

4 Check the liquid and, if dry, add more liquid as required until the rice is cooked, but not mushy. Just before serving, stir in the butter, white wine, tomatoes and olives and check the seasoning. Serve hot, garnished with thyme sprigs.

Risotto with Parmesan

This traditional risotto is simply flavoured with Parmesan cheese and golden fried onion.

INGREDIENTS

Serves 3–4
1.2 litres/2 pints/5 cups beef, chicken
   or vegetable stock
65g/2½oz/5 tbsp butter
1 small onion, finely chopped
275g/10oz/scant 1½ cups risotto rice
120ml/4fl oz/½ cup dry white wine
75g/3oz/⅓ cup freshly grated
   Parmesan cheese
salt and ground black pepper

1 Heat the stock in a saucepan, and leave to simmer until needed.

2 In a large heavy-based frying pan, melt two-thirds of the butter. Stir in the onion, and cook gently until soft and golden.

3 Add the rice, mixing well to coat with butter. After 1–2 minutes, pour in the white wine. Raise the heat slightly, and cook until the wine evaporates. Add one small ladleful of the hot stock. Cook until the stock is absorbed, stirring the rice with a wooden spoon to prevent it from sticking to the pan. Add a little more stock, and stir until the rice dries out again. Continue stirring and adding the liquid a little at a time. After about 20 minutes of cooking time, taste the rice and season as necessary.

4 Continue cooking, stirring and adding the liquid until the rice is *al dente*. The total cooking time of the risotto may be from 20–35 minutes. If you run out of stock, use hot water, but do not worry if the rice is done before you have used up all the stock.

5 Remove the pan from the heat. Stir in the remaining butter and the Parmesan cheese. Taste again for seasoning. Allow the risotto to rest for 3–4 minutes before serving.

Prawn Risotto

The soft pink colour of this prawn risotto comes from the addition of a little tomato purée.

INGREDIENTS

Serves 4
350g/12oz fresh prawns in the shell
1.2 litres/2 pints/5 cups water
1 bay leaf
1–2 sprigs parsley
5ml/1 tsp whole black peppercorns
2 garlic cloves, peeled
65g/2½oz/5 tbsp butter
2 shallots, finely chopped
275g/10oz/scant 1½ cups risotto rice
15ml/1 tbsp tomato purée with
   120ml/4fl oz/½ cup dry white wine
salt and ground black pepper

1 Place the prawns in a large saucepan with the water, herbs, peppercorns and garlic. Bring to the boil and cook for about 4 minutes. Remove the prawns, peel them, and return the shells to the saucepan. Boil the shells for another 10 minutes. Strain. Return the stock to the saucepan, and simmer until needed.

2 Slice the prawns in half lengthways, removing the dark vein along the back. Set 4 halves aside for garnish, and roughly chop the rest.

3 Heat two-thirds of the butter in a casserole. Add the shallots and cook until golden. Stir in the prawns and cook for a further 1–2 minutes.

4 Add the rice, mixing well to coat with butter. After 1–2 minutes pour in the tomato purée and wine mixture. Follow steps 3–5 for Risotto with Parmesan, omitting the cheese and garnishing the finished risotto with the reserved prawn halves.

African Lamb and Vegetable Pilau

INGREDIENTS

Serves 4

For the meat curry

450g/1lb boned shoulder of lamb
2.5ml/½ tsp dried thyme
2.5ml/½ tsp paprika
5ml/1 tsp garam masala
1 garlic clove, crushed
25ml/1½ tbsp vegetable oil
900ml/1½ pints/3¾ cups lamb stock
salt and ground black pepper

For the rice

30ml/2 tbsp butter or margarine
1 onion, chopped
175g/6oz/1 cup diced potato
1 carrot, sliced
½ red pepper, seeded and chopped
115g/4oz/1 cup sliced green cabbage
1 green chilli, seeded and chopped
60ml/4 tbsp natural yogurt
2.5ml/½ tsp ground cumin
5 green cardamom pods
2 garlic cloves, crushed
350g/12oz/scant 1½ cups basmati rice
about 50g/2oz/¼ cup cashew nuts
salt and ground black pepper

1 First make the meat curry. Place the lamb in a large bowl and add the thyme, paprika, garam masala, garlic and salt and pepper. Stir, cover, and leave in a cool place for 2–3 hours.

2 Heat the oil in a large saucepan and fry the lamb over a moderate heat for 5–6 minutes, until browned.

3 Add the stock, stir, then cook, covered, for 35–40 minutes. Transfer the lamb to a bowl and pour the liquid into a measuring jug, topping up with water if necessary, to make 600ml/1 pint/2½ cups.

4 To make the rice, melt the butter or margarine and fry the onion, potato and carrot for 5 minutes.

5 Add the red pepper, cabbage, chilli, yogurt, spices, garlic and the reserved meat stock. Stir well, cover, then simmer gently for 5–10 minutes, until the cabbage has wilted.

6 Stir in the rice and lamb, cover and simmer over a low heat for 20 minutes or until the rice is cooked. Sprinkle in the cashew nuts and season to taste with salt and pepper. Serve hot.

Nasi Goreng

One of the most popular and well-known Indonesian dishes, this is a marvellous way to use up leftover rice, chicken and meats such as pork.

INGREDIENTS

Serves 4–6

350g/12oz/scant 1½ cups dry weight
  basmati rice, cooked and cooled
2 eggs
30ml/2 tbsp water
105ml/7 tbsp oil
225g/8oz pork fillet or fillet of beef
2–3 fresh red chillies, seeded and sliced
1cm/½ in cube terasi (shrimp paste)
2 garlic cloves, crushed
1 onion, sliced
115g/4oz/1 cup cooked, peeled prawns
225g/8oz/1½ cups cooked
  chicken, chopped
30ml/2 tbsp dark soy sauce or
  45–60ml/3–4 tbsp tomato ketchup
salt and ground black pepper
celery leaves, deep-fried onions and
  coriander sprigs, to garnish

1 Separate the grains of the cooked and cooled rice with a fork. Cover and set aside until needed.

2 Beat the eggs with the water and season lightly. Make two or three thin omelettes in a frying pan, with a minimum of oil and leave to cool. When cold, roll up each omelette and cut into strips. Set aside.

3 Cut the pork or beef fillet into neat strips. Finely shred one of the chillies and set aside.

4 Put the terasi, with the remaining chilli, the garlic and onion, in a food processor, or use a pestle and mortar, and grind to a fine paste.

5 Heat the remaining oil in a wok and fry the paste, without browning, until it gives off a rich, spicy aroma. Add the pork or beef, tossing the meat all the time, to seal in the juices. Cook for 2 minutes, stirring constantly. Add the prawns, cook for 2 minutes and then stir in the chicken, cold rice, dark soy sauce or ketchup and season to taste. Stir all the time to keep the rice light and fluffy and prevent it from sticking.

6 Turn onto a hot serving plate and garnish with the omelette strips, celery leaves, onions, reserved shredded chilli and the coriander sprigs.

Chinese Fried Rice

INGREDIENTS

Serves 4–6

2 eggs
45ml/3 tbsp vegetable oil
4 shallots or 1 onion, finely chopped
5ml/1 tsp finely chopped fresh
    root ginger
1 garlic clove, crushed
225g/8oz/2 cups prawns
5–10ml/1–2 tsp chilli sauce (optional)
3 spring onions, green parts only,
    roughly chopped
225g/8oz/2 cups frozen peas
225g/8oz thickly sliced roast
    pork, diced
45ml/3 tbsp light soy sauce
350g/12oz/scant 1½ cups dry weight
    long grain rice, cooked
salt and ground black pepper

1 In a bowl, beat the eggs well, and season. Heat 15ml/1 tbsp of the oil in a large non-stick frying pan, pour in the eggs and cook until just set. Roll up the pancake, cut into thin strips and set aside until needed.

2 Heat the remaining oil in a wok, add the shallots or onion, ginger, garlic and prawns and cook for about 1–2 minutes. Do not let the garlic burn.

3 Add the chilli sauce, spring onions, peas, pork and soy sauce, and stir to heat through. Add the rice and fry over a moderate heat for 6–8 minutes. Turn into a dish and decorate with the pancake. Season to taste.

Chicken with Garlicky Rice

Chicken wings, when cooked until really tender, have a surprising amount of meat on them, and make a very economical supper.

INGREDIENTS

Serves 4

1 large onion, chopped
2 garlic cloves, crushed
30ml/2 tbsp sunflower oil
175g/6oz/scant 1 cup patna or
    basmati rice
350ml/12fl oz/1½ cups hot
    chicken stock
10ml/2 tsp finely grated lemon rind
30ml/2 tbsp chopped fresh mixed herbs
8 or 12 chicken wings
50g/2oz/¼ cup plain flour
salt and ground black pepper
coriander sprigs, to garnish

1 Preheat the oven to 200°C/400°F/ Gas 6. Fry the onion and garlic in the oil in a large ovenproof pan until soft and golden. Add the rice and toss until well coated in oil.

2 Stir in the stock, lemon rind and herbs and bring to the boil. Cover and cook in the centre of the oven for 40–50 minutes. Stir the rice once or twice during cooking.

3 Meanwhile, pat the chicken wings dry. Season the flour and use it to coat the chicken wings thoroughly, dusting off any excess.

4 Place the chicken wings in a small roasting tin and cook in the top of the oven for 30–40 minutes, turning once, until crispy and golden.

5 Serve the rice and the chicken wings, garnished with coriander, with a fresh tomato sauce and a selection of vegetables.

Rice and Broad Bean Meatballs

These tasty beef koftas make a delightful change from ordinary meatballs.

Ingredients

Serves 4

115g/4oz/generous ½ cup long
  grain rice
450g/1lb minced lean beef
115g/4oz/1½ cup plain flour
3 eggs, beaten
115g/4oz/1½ cup broad beans, skinned
30ml/2 tbsp chopped fresh dill
25g/1oz/2 tbsp butter or margarine
1 large onion, chopped
2.5ml/½ tsp ground turmeric
1.2 litres/2 pints/5 cups water
salt and ground black pepper
chopped fresh parsley, to garnish
naan bread, to serve

1 Put the rice in a pan of water and boil for about 4 minutes until half cooked. Drain and place in a bowl with the meat, flour, eggs and seasoning. Knead until well blended.

--- Cook's Tip ---

If fresh broad beans are unavailable, replace them with frozen broad beans, defrosted before use.

2 Add the skinned broad beans and dill and knead again until the mixture is firm and pasty. Shape the mixture into large balls and set aside on a plate in a cool place.

3 Melt the butter or margarine in a large saucepan or flameproof casserole and fry the chopped onion for 3–4 minutes until golden. Stir in the turmeric, cook for 30 seconds and then add the water and bring to the boil.

4 Add the meatballs to the pan, then simmer for 45–60 minutes until the gravy is reduced to about 250ml/ 8fl oz/1 cup. Garnish with the chopped parsley and serve with naan bread.

French Beans, Rice and Beef

INGREDIENTS

Serves 4

25g/1oz/2 tbsp butter or margarine
1 large onion, chopped
450g/1lb stewing beef, cubed
2 garlic cloves, crushed
5ml/1 tsp ground cinnamon
5ml/1 tsp ground cumin
5ml/1 tsp ground turmeric
450g/1lb tomatoes, chopped
30ml/2 tbsp tomato purée
350ml/12fl oz/1½ cups water
350g/12oz/2½ cups French
   beans, trimmed and halved
salt and ground black pepper

For the rice

275g/10oz/scant 1½ cups basmati rice,
   soaked in salted water for 2 hours
1.75 litres/3 pints/7½ cups water
45ml/3 tbsp melted butter
2–3 saffron strands, soaked in
   15ml/1 tbsp boiling water
pinch of salt

1 Melt the butter or margarine in a large saucepan or flameproof casserole and fry the onion until golden. Add the beef and fry until evenly browned, then add the garlic, spices, tomatoes, tomato purée and water. Season with salt and pepper. Bring to the boil, then simmer over a low heat for about 30 minutes.

2 Add the French beans and continue cooking for a further 15 minutes until the meat is tender and most of the meat juices have evaporated.

3 Meanwhile, prepare the rice. Drain, then boil it in salted water for about 5 minutes. Reduce the heat and simmer very gently for 10 minutes or until it is half-cooked. Drain, and rinse the rice in warm water. Wash and dry the saucepan.

4 Heat 15ml/1 tbsp of the melted butter in the pan and stir in about a third of the rice. Spoon half of the meat mixture over the rice, add a layer of rice, then the remaining meat and finish with another layer of rice.

5 Pour the remaining melted butter over the rice and cover the pan with a clean dish towel. Secure with the lid and then steam the rice for 30–45 minutes over a low heat.

6 Take 45ml/3 tbsp of cooked rice from the pan and mix with the saffron water. Serve the cooked rice and beef on a large dish and sprinkle the saffron rice on top.

Yogurt Chicken and Rice

This is flavoured with *zereshk*, small dried berries available from Middle Eastern stores.

INGREDIENTS

Serves 6
40g/1½ oz/3 tbsp butter
1.5kg/3–3½ lb chicken pieces
1 large onion, chopped
250ml/8fl oz/1 cup chicken stock
2 eggs
475ml/16fl oz/2 cups natural yogurt
2–3 saffron strands, dissolved in 15ml/
   1 tbsp boiling water
5ml/1 tsp ground cinnamon
450g/1lb/generous 2¼ cups basmati
   rice, soaked in salted water
   for 2 hours
75g/3oz *zereshk*
salt and ground black pepper
herb salad, to serve

1 Melt two-thirds of the butter in a casserole and fry the chicken and onion for 4–5 minutes, until the onion is softened and the chicken browned.

2 Add the stock and salt and pepper, bring to the boil and then simmer for 45 minutes, or until the chicken is cooked and the stock reduced by half.

3 Skin and bone the chicken. Cut the flesh into large pieces and place in a large bowl. Reserve the stock.

4 Beat the eggs and blend with the yogurt. Add the saffron water and cinnamon and season with salt and pepper. Pour over the chicken and leave to marinate on one side for up to 2 hours.

5 Drain the rice and then boil in salted water for 5 minutes, reduce the heat and simmer very gently for 10 minutes, until half cooked. Drain and rinse in warm water.

6 Transfer the chicken from the yogurt mixture to a dish and mix half the rice into the yogurt.

7 Preheat the oven to 160°C/325°F/ Gas 3 and grease a large 10cm/4in deep ovenproof dish.

8 Place the rice and yogurt mixture in the bottom of the dish, arrange the chicken pieces in a layer on top and then add the plain rice. Warm the *zereshk* thoroughly, then sprinkle over.

9 Mix the remaining butter with the chicken stock and pour over the rice. Cover tightly with foil and cook in the oven for 35–45 minutes.

10 Leave the dish to cool for a few minutes. Place on a cold, damp dish towel which will help lift the rice from the base of the dish, then run a knife around the inside edge of the dish. Place a large flat plate over the dish and turn out. You should have a rice "cake" which can be cut into wedges. Serve hot with a herb salad.

Louisiana Rice

Aubergine and pork combine with herbs and spices to make a highly flavoursome dish.

INGREDIENTS

Serves 4

60ml/4 tbsp vegetable oil
1 small aubergine, diced
225g/8oz minced pork
1 green pepper, seeded and chopped
2 sticks celery, chopped
1 onion, chopped
1 garlic clove, crushed
5ml/1 tsp cayenne pepper
5ml/1 tsp paprika
5ml/1 tsp black pepper
2.5ml/½ tsp salt
5ml/1 tsp dried thyme
2.5ml/½ tsp dried oregano
475ml/16fl oz/2 cups chicken stock
225g/8oz chicken livers, minced
150g/5oz/scant ⅔ cup long grain rice
1 bay leaf
45ml/3 tbsp chopped fresh parsley
celery leaves, to garnish

1 Heat the oil in a frying pan until piping hot, then add the aubergine and stir-fry for about 5 minutes.

2 Add the pork and cook for 6–8 minutes until browned, using a wooden spoon to break up any lumps.

3 Add the green pepper, celery, onion, garlic and all the spices and herbs. Cover and cook over a high heat for 5–6 minutes, stirring frequently from the base of the pan to scrape up and distribute the crispy brown bits.

4 Pour in the chicken stock and stir to remove any sediment from the base of the pan. Cover and cook for 6 minutes over a moderate heat. Stir in the chicken livers, cook for 2 minutes, then stir in the rice and add the bay leaf.

5 Reduce the heat, cover and simmer for 6–7 minutes. Turn off the heat and leave to stand for a further 10–15 minutes until the rice is tender. Remove the bay leaf and stir in the chopped parsley. Serve the rice hot, garnished with the celery leaves.

EASY ENTERTAINING

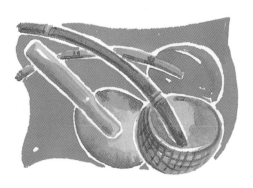

*When a crowd is expected, but table
space and budgets are tight, meals based
on light, aromatic rice are sure to fit the
bill. Rice is highly absorbent and so
enhances many exotic flavours, from
spices and herbs through to Oriental
sauces. It keeps warm without spoiling,
and all these dishes can be made ahead
of time and reheated as guests arrive –
ready for simple serving and eating
with a fork. A good serving tip is to
mound rice dishes high on large serving
platters and garnish with fresh herbs,
brown fried onion, strips of chilli or
maybe wedges of lemon and lime. This
looks far more attractive then spooning
into deep-sided bowls.*

Smoked Trout Pilaff

Smoked trout might seem an unusual partner for rice, but this is a winning combination.

INGREDIENTS

Serves 4

225g/8oz/generous 1 cup basmati rice
40g/1½oz/3 tbsp butter
2 onions, sliced into rings
1 garlic clove, crushed
2 bay leaves
2 whole cloves
2 green cardamom pods
2.5cm/2in cinnamon sticks
5ml/1 tsp cumin seeds
4 hot-smoked trout fillets, skinned
50g/2oz/½ cup slivered
   almonds, toasted
50g/2oz/scant ½ cup seedless raisins
30ml/2 tbsp chopped fresh parsley
mango chutney and poppadums,
   to serve

1 Wash the rice thoroughly in several changes of water and drain well. Set aside. Melt the butter in a large frying pan and fry the onions until well browned, stirring frequently.

2 Add the garlic, bay leaves, cloves, cardamom pods, cinnamon and cumin seeds and stir-fry for 1 minute.

3 Stir in the rice, then add 600ml/ 1 pint/2½ cups boiling water. Bring to the boil. Cover the pan tightly, reduce the heat and cook very gently for 20–25 minutes, until the water has been absorbed and the rice is tender.

4 Flake the smoked trout and add to the pan with the almonds and raisins. Fork through gently. Cover the pan and allow the smoked trout to warm in the rice for a few minutes. Scatter over the parsley and serve with mango chutney and poppadums.

Seafood Paella

This is a great dish to serve to guests. Bring the pan to the table and let everyone help themselves.

INGREDIENTS

Serves 4

60ml/4 tbsp olive oil
225g/8oz monkfish or cod, skinned and cut into chunks
3 prepared baby squid, body cut into rings and tentacles chopped
1 red mullet, filleted, skinned and cut into chunks (optional)
1 onion, chopped
3 garlic cloves, finely chopped
1 red pepper, seeded and sliced
4 tomatoes, skinned and chopped
225g/8oz/generous 1 cup risotto rice
450ml/³/₄ pint/1⁷/₈ cups fish stock
150ml/¹/₄ pint/²/₃ cup white wine
75g/3oz/¹/₃ cup frozen peas
4–5 saffron strands soaked in 30ml/ 2 tbsp hot water
115g/4oz/1 cup cooked peeled prawns
8 fresh mussels in the shell, scrubbed
salt and ground black pepper
15ml/1 tbsp chopped fresh parsley, to garnish
lemon wedges, to serve

1 Heat 30ml/2 tbsp of the oil in a large frying pan and add the monkfish or cod, the squid and the red mullet, if using. Stir-fry for 2 minutes, then transfer the fish to a bowl with all the juices and reserve on one side.

2 Heat the remaining 30ml/2 tbsp of oil in the pan and add the onion, garlic and pepper. Fry for 6–7 minutes, stirring frequently, until softened.

3 Stir in the tomatoes and fry for 2 minutes, then add the rice, stirring to coat the grains with oil, and cook for 2–3 minutes. Pour over the fish stock and wine and add the peas and saffron water. Season well and mix.

4 Gently stir in the reserved cooked fish with all the juices, followed by the prawns. Push the mussels into the rice. Cover and cook over a gentle heat for about 30 minutes, or until the stock has been absorbed but the rice mixture is still relatively moist.

5 Remove from the heat, keep covered and leave the paella to stand for 5 minutes. Sprinkle with parsley and serve the paella with the lemon wedges.

Chicken Biryani

INGREDIENTS

Serves 4

275g/10oz/scant 1½ cups basmati rice
2.5ml/½ tsp salt
5 whole green cardamom pods
2–3 whole cloves
5cm/2in cinnamon stick
45ml/3 tbsp vegetable oil
3 onions, sliced
4 x 175g/6oz chicken breasts, cubed
1.5ml/¼ tsp ground cloves
5 green cardamom pods, seeds ground
1.5ml/¼ tsp hot chilli powder
5ml/1 tsp ground cumin
5ml/1 tsp ground coriander
2.5ml/½ tsp ground black pepper
3 garlic cloves, chopped
5ml/1 tsp finely chopped fresh
   root ginger
juice of 1 lemon
4 tomatoes, sliced
30ml/2 tbsp chopped fresh coriander
150ml/¼ pint/⅔ cup natural yogurt
4–5 saffron strands soaked in 10ml/
   2 tsp hot milk
45ml/3 tbsp toasted flaked almonds and
   fresh coriander sprigs, to garnish
natural yogurt, to serve

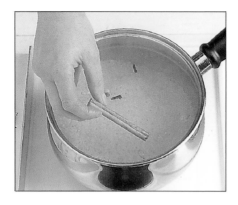

1 Preheat the oven to 190°C/375°F/ Gas 5. Bring a large pan of water to the boil and add the rice, salt, whole cardamom pods, cloves and cinnamon stick. Boil for 2 minutes then drain, leaving the whole spices in the rice.

2 Heat the oil in a pan and fry the onions for 8 minutes, until browned and softened. Add the chicken, followed by all the ground spices, the garlic, ginger and lemon juice. Stir-fry for 5 minutes.

3 Transfer the chicken mixture to an ovenproof casserole and lay the tomatoes on top. Sprinkle on the fresh coriander, spoon over the yogurt and top with the drained rice.

4 Drizzle the saffron milk over the rice and pour over about 150ml/ ¼ pint/⅔ cup of water.

5 Cover tightly and bake in the oven for 1 hour. Transfer to a warmed serving platter and remove the whole spices from the rice. Garnish with toasted almonds and fresh coriander sprigs and serve with natural yogurt.

Joloff Chicken and Rice

This well-known, colourful West African rice dish is always a big hit at dinner parties.

INGREDIENTS

Serves 4

1kg/2¼lb chicken, cut into 4–6 pieces
2 garlic cloves, crushed
5ml/1 tsp dried thyme
30ml/2 tbsp palm or vegetable oil
400g/14oz can chopped tomatoes
15ml/1 tbsp tomato purée
1 onion, chopped
450ml/¾ pint/1⅞ cups chicken stock
    or water
30ml/2 tbsp dried shrimps or
    crayfish, ground
1 green chilli, seeded and
    finely chopped
350g/12oz/scant 1½ cups long grain
    rice, washed

1 Rub the chicken with the garlic and thyme and set aside.

2 Heat the oil in a saucepan until hazy and then add the chopped tomatoes, tomato purée and onion. Cook over a moderately high heat for about 15 minutes until the tomatoes are well reduced, stirring occasionally at first and then more frequently as the tomatoes thicken.

3 Reduce the heat a little, add the chicken pieces and stir well to coat with the sauce. Cook for 10 minutes, stirring, then add the stock or water, the dried shrimps or crayfish and the chilli. Bring to the boil and simmer for 5 minutes, stirring occasionally.

4 Put the rice in a separate saucepan. Scoop 300ml/½ pint/1¼ cups of the sauce into a measuring jug, top up with water to 450ml/¾ pint/1⅞ cups and stir the liquid into the rice.

5 Cook, covered, until the liquid is absorbed, then place a piece of foil on top of the rice, cover the pan with a lid and cook over a low heat for 20 minutes until the rice is cooked, adding a little more water if necessary.

6 Transfer the chicken pieces to a warmed serving plate. Simmer the sauce until reduced by half. Pour over the chicken and serve with the rice.

Special Fried Rice

This delicious recipe combines a mixture of chicken, shrimps and vegetables with fried rice. Lettuce and a sprinkling of nuts are added for extra crunch.

INGREDIENTS

Serves 4

175g/6oz/scant 1 cup long grain
   white rice
45ml/3 tbsp groundnut oil
1 garlic clove, crushed
4 spring onions, finely chopped
115g/4oz/1 cup diced cooked chicken
115g/4oz/1 cup cooked peeled
   shrimps (rinsed if canned)
50g/2oz/½ cup frozen peas
1 egg, beaten with a pinch of salt
50g/2oz/1 cup shredded lettuce
30ml/2 tbsp light soy sauce
pinch of caster sugar
salt and ground black pepper
15ml/1 tbsp chopped, roasted cashew
   nuts, to garnish

1 Rinse the rice in two to three changes of warm water to wash away some of the starch. Drain well.

2 Put the rice in a saucepan and add 15ml/1 tbsp of the oil and 350ml/12fl oz/1½ cups water. Cover and bring to the boil, stir once, then cover and simmer for 12–15 minutes, until nearly all the water has been absorbed. Turn off the heat and leave, covered, to stand for 10 minutes. Fluff up with a fork and leave to cool.

3 Heat the remaining oil in a wok, add the garlic and spring onions and stir-fry for 30 seconds.

4 Add the chicken, shrimps and peas and stir-fry for 1–2 minutes, then add the cooked rice and stir-fry for a further 2 minutes. Pour in the egg and stir-fry until just set. Stir in the lettuce, soy sauce, sugar and seasoning. Transfer to a warmed serving bowl, sprinkle with the chopped cashew nuts and serve immediately.

Seafood Pilaff

INGREDIENTS

Serves 4

10ml/2 tsp olive oil
250g/9oz/1¼ cups long grain rice
5ml/1 tsp ground turmeric
1 red pepper, seeded and diced
1 small onion, finely chopped
2 courgettes, sliced
150g/5oz/scant 2 cups button
   mushrooms, halved
150ml/12fl oz/1½ cups fish or
   chicken stock
150ml/¼ pint/⅔ cup dry white wine
350g/12oz white fish fillets
12 fresh mussels in the shell (or cooked
   shelled mussels)
salt and ground black pepper
grated rind of 1 orange, to garnish

1 Heat the oil in a large, non-stick frying pan and fry the rice and turmeric gently for about 1 minute.

2 Add the pepper, onion, courgettes, and mushrooms. Stir in the stock and wine. Bring to the boil.

3 Reduce the heat and add the fish. Cover and simmer gently for about 15 minutes, until the rice is tender and the liquid absorbed. Stir in the mussels and heat thoroughly. Adjust the seasoning, sprinkle with the grated orange rind and serve hot.

Stuffed Spring Chickens

This dish is widely found in the Lebanon and Syria. The stuffing is a delicious blend of meat, nuts and rice.

INGREDIENTS

Serves 6–8
2 x 1kg/2¼ lb chickens
15ml/1 tbsp butter
natural yogurt and salad, to serve

For the stuffing

45ml/3 tbsp oil
1 onion, chopped
450g/1lb minced lamb
75g/3oz/1 cup almonds, chopped
75g/3oz/1 cup pine nuts
350g/12oz/scant 1½ cups dry weight rice, cooked
salt and ground black pepper

1 Preheat the oven to180°C/350°F/ Gas 4. Remove the giblets, if necessary, from the chickens and rinse the body cavities in cold water.

2 For the stuffing, heat the oil in a large frying pan and sauté the onion until slightly softened. Add the minced lamb and cook over a moderate heat for 4–8 minutes until well browned, stirring frequently. Set aside.

3 Heat a small pan over a moderate heat and dry-fry the almonds and pine nuts for 2–3 minutes until golden, shaking the pan frequently.

4 Mix together the meat mixture, almonds, pine nuts and cooked rice. Season with salt and pepper, and then spoon the mixture into the body cavities of the chickens. Rub the chickens all over with the butter.

5 Place the chickens in a large roasting dish, cover with foil and bake in the oven for 45–60 minutes. After about 30 minutes, remove the foil and baste the chickens with the pan juices. Continue cooking without the foil until the chickens are cooked through and the meat juices run clear. Serve the chickens, cut into portions, with yogurt and a salad.

Festive Rice

This Thai dish is traditionally served shaped into a cone and surrounded by a variety of accompaniments.

INGREDIENTS

Serves 8

450g/1lb/generous 2¼ cups Thai fragrant rice
60ml/4 tbsp oil
2 garlic cloves, crushed
2 onions, finely sliced
5cm/2in fresh turmeric, peeled and crushed
750ml/1¼ pints/3 cups water
400ml/14fl oz can coconut milk
1–2 lemon grass stems, bruised

For the accompaniments
omelette strips
2 fresh red chillies, shredded
cucumber chunks
tomato wedges
deep-fried onions
prawn crackers

1 Wash the rice in several changes of water. Drain well.

2 Heat the oil in a wok and gently fry the garlic, onions and turmeric for a few minutes, until they are softened but not browned.

3 Add the rice and stir well so that each grain is thoroughly coated. Pour in the water and coconut milk and add the lemon grass.

4 Bring to the boil, stirring well. Cover the pan and cook gently for 15–20 minutes, or until all of the liquid has been completely absorbed.

5 Remove the pan from the heat. Cover with a clean dish towel, put on the lid and leave to stand in a warm place for 15 minutes.

6 Remove the lemon grass, turn out on to a serving platter and garnish the dish with the accompaniments.

Seafood and Rice

INGREDIENTS

Serves 4

30ml/2 tbsp oil
115g/4oz smoked bacon, rind
   removed, diced
1 onion, chopped
2 sticks celery, chopped
2 large garlic cloves, chopped
5ml/1 tsp cayenne pepper
2 bay leaves
5ml/1 tsp dried oregano
2.5ml/½ tsp dried thyme
4 tomatoes, peeled and chopped
150ml/¼ pint/⅔ cup tomato sauce
350g/12oz/scant 1 cup long grain rice
475ml/16fl oz/2 cups fish stock
175g/6oz cod, or haddock, skinned,
   boned and cubed
115g/4oz/1 cup cooked,
   peeled prawns
salt and ground black pepper
2 spring onions, chopped, to garnish

1 Preheat the oven to 180°C/350°F/ Gas 4. Heat the oil in a large saucepan and fry the bacon until crisp. Add the onion and celery and stir until beginning to stick to the pan.

2 Add the garlic, cayenne pepper, herbs, tomatoes and seasoning and mix well. Stir in the tomato sauce, rice and stock and bring to the boil

3 Gently stir in the fish and transfer to an ovenproof dish. Cover tightly with foil and bake for 20–30 minutes, until the rice is just tender. Stir in the prawns and heat through. Serve sprinkled with the spring onions.

Chicken Jambalaya

INGREDIENTS

Serves 10

2 x 1.5kg/3–3½lb chickens
450g/1lb raw smoked gammon
50g/2oz/4 tbsp lard or bacon fat
50g/2oz/½ cup plain flour
3 onions, finely sliced
2 green peppers, seeded and sliced
675g/1½lb tomatoes, chopped
2–3 garlic cloves, crushed
10ml/2 tsp chopped fresh thyme or
   5ml/1 tsp dried thyme
24 Mediterranean prawns, peeled
500g/1¼lb/scant 3 cups long
   grain rice
2–3 dashes Tabasco sauce
6 spring onions, finely chopped
45ml/3 tbsp fresh parsley, chopped
salt and ground black pepper

1 Cut each chicken into 10 pieces and season. Dice the gammon, discarding the rind and fat.

2 In a large casserole, melt the lard or bacon fat and brown the chicken pieces all over, lifting them out and setting them aside as they are done.

3 Turn the heat down, sprinkle the flour onto the fat in the pan and stir until the roux turns golden brown.

4 Return the chicken pieces to the pan, add the diced gammon, onions, green peppers, tomatoes, garlic and thyme and cook, stirring regularly, for 10 minutes, then stir in the prawns.

5 Stir the rice into the pan with one- and-a-half times the rice's volume in cold water. Season with salt, pepper and Tabasco sauce. Bring to the boil and cook over a gentle heat until the rice is tender and the liquid absorbed. Add a little extra boiling water if the rice dries out before it is cooked.

6 Mix the spring onions and parsley into the finished dish, reserving a little of the mixture to scatter over the jambalaya. Serve hot.

VEGETARIAN DISHES

Rice and vegetarian foods are natural partners. Many rice-eating cultures have a wealth of delicious non-meat recipes, in fact all of the world's oldest vegetarian religious sects have some of the most exciting rice recipes. Nutritionally, it makes sense to serve rice with a good selection of vegetables, nuts and pulses in a meal – each individual food has differing amino acid proteins, so by combining a mixture you are completing the circle of top class protein. It is also a great way to stay healthy and enjoy good food.

Wild Rice Rösti

Rösti is a traditional dish from Switzerland. This variation has the extra nuttiness of wild rice and a bright simple sauce as a fresh accompaniment.

INGREDIENTS

Serves 6

50g/2oz/¼ cup wild rice
900g/2lb large potatoes
45ml/3 tbsp walnut oil
5ml/1 tsp yellow mustard seeds
1 onion, coarsely grated and drained
   in a sieve
30ml/2 tbsp fresh thyme leaves
salt and ground black pepper

For the purée

350g/12oz/2 cups carrots, peeled and
   roughly chopped
rind and juice of 1 large orange

1 For the purée, place the carrots in a saucepan, cover with cold water and add 2 pieces of orange rind. Bring to the boil and cook for 10 minutes, or until the carrots are tender. Drain thoroughly and discard the rind.

2 Purée the carrots in a blender with 60ml/4 tbsp of the orange juice. Return to the pan to reheat.

3 Place the wild rice in a clean pan and cover with water. Bring to the boil and cook for 30–40 minutes, until the rice is just starting to split, but still crunchy. Drain and put to one side.

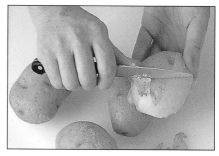

4 Scrub the potatoes, place in a large pan and cover with cold water. Bring to the boil and cook for 10–15 minutes, until just tender. Drain well and leave to cool slightly. When the potatoes are cool, peel and coarsely grate them into a large bowl. Add the cooked wild rice and stir.

5 Heat 30ml/2 tbsp of the walnut oil in a non-stick frying pan and add the mustard seeds. When they start to pop, add the onion and cook gently for 5 minutes, until softened. Add to the potato and rice mixture, together with the thyme, and mix thoroughly. Season to taste with salt and pepper.

6 Heat the remaining oil in the frying pan and add the potato mixture. Press down well and cook for 10 minutes, or until golden brown. Cover the pan with a plate and flip over, then slide the rösti back into the pan for another 10 minutes to cook the other side. Serve with the reheated carrot and orange purée.

Golden Vegetable Paella

Add some chopped fresh coriander or flat-leaf parsley to this colourful paella for even more colour contrast.

INGREDIENTS

Serves 4

pinch of saffron strands or 5ml/1 tsp
    ground turmeric
750ml/1¼ pints/3 cups hot
    vegetable stock
90ml/6 tbsp olive oil
2 large onions, sliced
3 garlic cloves, chopped
275g/10oz/scant 1½ cups long
    grain rice
50g/2oz/⅓ cup wild rice
175g/6oz pumpkin or butternut
    squash, chopped
175g/6oz carrots, cut into matchsticks
1 yellow pepper, seeded and sliced
4 tomatoes, peeled and chopped
115g/4oz/scant 2 cups oyster
    mushrooms, quartered
salt and ground black pepper
strips of red, yellow and green pepper,
    to garnish

1 Place the saffron in a small bowl with 45–60ml/3–4 tbsp boiling stock. Leave to stand for 5 minutes. Meanwhile, heat the oil in a paella pan or large heavy-based frying pan. Fry the onions and garlic gently until just softening. If using turmeric, add it to the onions and garlic in the pan.

2 Add the rices and toss for 2–3 minutes until coated in oil. Add the stock to the pan with the pumpkin or squash, together with the saffron liquid. Stir as it comes to the boil and reduce the heat to the minimum.

—————— COOK'S TIP ——————

To peel pumpkin or butternut squash, first chop the vegetable into several manageable pieces, discarding any seeds and pith, then peel with a pantry knife or an ordinary vegetable peeler.

3 Cover with a pan lid or foil and cook very gently for about 15 minutes. (Avoid stirring unneccesarily as this lets out the steam.) Add the carrots, yellow pepper, tomatoes, salt and black pepper, cover again and leave for a further 5 minutes, or until the rice is almost tender to the bite.

4 Finally, add the oyster mushrooms, check the seasoning and cook, uncovered, for just enough time to soften the mushrooms without letting the paella stick. Top with the peppers and serve as soon as possible.

Stir-fry Nutty Rice

INGREDIENTS

Serves 4

½ cucumber
2 spring onions, sliced
1 garlic clove, crushed
2 carrots, thinly sliced
1 small red or yellow pepper, seeded
  and sliced
45ml/3 tbsp sunflower or
  groundnut oil
¼ small green cabbage, shredded
225g/8oz/4 cups cooked long
  grain rice
30ml/2 tbsp light soy sauce
15ml/1 tbsp sesame oil
chopped fresh parsley or
  coriander (optional)
115g/4oz/2 cups unsalted cashew nuts,
  almonds or peanuts
salt and ground black pepper

1 Halve the cucumber lengthways and scoop out the seeds with a teaspoon. Slice the flesh diagonally, then set aside until needed.

2 In a wok or large frying pan, stir-fry the onions, garlic, carrots and pepper in the oil for about 3 minutes until they are just soft.

3 Add the cabbage and cucumber and fry for another 1–2 minutes until the leaves just begin to wilt. Mix in the rice, soy sauce, sesame oil and seasoning. Heat the mixture through, stirring and tossing all the time.

4 Add the herbs, if desired, and the nuts. Check the seasoning and serve the rice piping hot.

Wild Rice with Grilled Vegetables

INGREDIENTS

Serves 4

225g/8oz/generous 1 cup mixed wild
  and long grain rice
1 large aubergine, thickly sliced
1 red, 1 yellow and 1 green pepper,
  seeded and cut into quarters
2 red onions, sliced
225g/8oz/generous 3 cups brown cap
  or shiitake mushrooms
2 small courgettes, cut in
  half lengthways
olive oil, for brushing
30ml/2 tbsp chopped fresh thyme

For the dressing

90ml/6 tbsp extra virgin olive oil
30ml/2 tbsp balsamic vinegar
2 garlic cloves, crushed
salt and ground black pepper

1 Put the rice in a pan of cold salted water. Bring to the boil, then reduce the heat, cover and cook gently for 30–40 minutes (or follow the packet instructions) until tender.

2 To make the dressing, mix together the olive oil, vinegar, garlic and seasoning in a bowl or screw-top jar until thoroughly blended. Set aside while you grill the vegetables.

3 Arrange the vegetables on a grill rack. Brush with olive oil and grill for 8–10 minutes until tender and well browned, turning them occasionally and brushing again with oil.

4 Drain the rice and toss in half the dressing. Tip into a serving dish and arrange the grilled vegetables on top. Pour over the remaining dressing and scatter over the chopped thyme.

Persian Rice with a Tahdeeg

Persian or Iranian cuisine is exotic and delicious, and the flavours are intense. A *tahdeeg* is the glorious, golden rice crust or "dig" that forms on the base of the saucepan.

INGREDIENTS

Serves 8

450g/1lb/generous 2¼ cups basmati
  rice, rinsed thoroughly and soaked
2 garlic cloves, crushed
2 onions, 1 chopped, 1 thinly sliced
150ml/¼ pint/⅔ cup sunflower oil
150g/5oz/⅔ cup green lentils, soaked
600ml/1 pint/2½ cups stock
50g/2oz/½ cup raisins
10ml/2 tsp ground coriander
45ml/3 tbsp tomato purée
a few saffron strands
1 egg yolk, beaten
10ml/2 tsp natural yogurt
75g/3oz/6 tbsp butter, melted
  and strained
extra oil, for frying
salt and ground black pepper

1 Drain the soaked rice, then cook it in plenty of boiling salted water for 3 minutes. Drain again.

2 In a large saucepan, fry the garlic and chopped onion in 30ml/2 tbsp oil for 5 minutes, then add the lentils, stock, raisins, coriander, tomato purée and seasoning. Bring to the boil, then cover and simmer for 20 minutes.

3 Soak the saffron strands in a little hot water. Remove about 120ml/8 tbsp of the cooked rice and mix with the egg yolk and yogurt. Season well.

4 In a large saucepan, heat about two-thirds of the remaining oil and scatter the egg and yogurt rice evenly over the base.

5 Scatter the remaining rice into the pan, alternating it with the lentil mixture. Build up in a pyramid shape away from the sides of the pan, finishing with plain rice on top.

6 With a long wooden spoon handle, make three holes down to the base of the pan and drizzle over the butter. Bring to a high heat, then wrap the pan lid in a clean, wet dish towel and place firmly on top. When a good head of steam appears, turn the heat down to low. Cook for about 30 minutes.

7 Meanwhile, fry the sliced onion in the remaining oil until browned and crisp. Drain well and set aside.

8 Remove the rice pan from the heat, still covered, and stand it briefly in a sink of cold water for a minute or two to loosen the base. Remove the lid and mix a few spoons of the white rice with the saffron water.

9 Toss the rice and lentils together in the pan and spoon out onto a serving dish in a mound. Scatter the saffron rice on top. Break up the rice crust on the pan base and place pieces of it around the mound. Scatter over the crispy fried onions and serve.

Broccoli Risotto Torte

This unusual savoury cake can be served hot or cold.

INGREDIENTS

Serves 6
225g/8oz broccoli, cut into very
   small florets
1 onion, chopped
2 garlic cloves, crushed
1 large yellow pepper, sliced
30ml/2 tbsp olive oil
50g/2oz/4 tbsp butter
225g/8oz/generous 1 cup risotto rice
120ml/4fl oz/½ cup dry white wine
1 litre/1¾ pints/4 cups stock
115g/4oz pecorino or Parmesan
   cheese, coarsely grated
4 eggs, separated
oil, for greasing
salt and ground black pepper
sliced tomato and chopped parsley,
   to garnish

1 Blanch the broccoli for 3 minutes then drain and reserve.

2 In a large saucepan, gently fry the onion, garlic and yellow pepper in the oil and butter for about 5 minutes until soft.

3 Stir in the rice, cook for 1 minute, then pour in the wine. Cook, stirring the mixture continuously, until the liquid is absorbed.

4 Pour in the stock and season well. Bring the rice to the boil then lower the heat to a simmer. Cook for 20 minutes, stirring occasionally.

5 Lightly grease a 25cm/10in round deep cake tin with a little oil and line the base of the tin with a disc of greaseproof paper. Preheat the oven to 180°C/350°F/Gas 4.

6 Stir the cheese into the rice, allow the mixture to cool for 5 minutes, then beat in the egg yolks. Add the broccoli and stir to mix.

7 Whisk the egg whites until they form soft peaks, then carefully fold them into the rice. Turn into the prepared tin and bake for about 1 hour until risen, golden brown and slightly wobbly in the centre.

8 Allow the torte to cool in the tin, then chill if serving cold. Run a knife round the edge of the tin and shake out onto a serving plate. If desired, garnish the torte with some sliced tomato and chopped parsley.

Kitchiri

INGREDIENTS

Serves 4

115g/4oz/1 cup green lentils
1 onion, chopped
1 garlic clove, crushed
50g/2oz/4 tbsp vegetarian ghee
  or butter
30ml/2 tbsp sunflower oil
225g/8oz/generous 1 cup easy-cook
  basmati rice
10ml/2 tsp ground coriander
10ml/2 tsp cumin seeds
2 cloves
3 green cardamom pods
2 bay leaves
5cm/2in cinnamon stick
1 litre/1³/₄ pints/4 cups stock
30ml/2 tbsp tomato purée
45ml/3 tbsp chopped fresh coriander
  or parsley
salt and ground black pepper

1 Cover the lentils with boiling water and soak for 30 minutes. Drain and boil them in fresh water for 10 minutes. Drain again and set aside.

2 Fry the onion and garlic in the ghee or butter and oil in a large saucepan for 5 minutes. Add the rice, stir well to coat the grains in the fat then stir in the spices. Cook gently for 1–2 minutes.

3 Add the lentils, stock, tomato purée and seasoning. Bring to the boil, cover and simmer for 20 minutes until the stock is absorbed and the lentils and rice are just soft. Stir in the fresh coriander or parsley and check the seasoning. Remove the cinnamon stick and bay leaves before serving.

Risotto Primavera

INGREDIENTS

Serves 4

1 litre/1³/₄ pints/4 cups vegetable stock
1 red onion, chopped
2 garlic cloves, crushed
30ml/2 tbsp olive oil
25g/1oz/2 tbsp butter
225g/8oz/generous 1 cup risotto rice
  (do not rinse)
45ml/3 tbsp dry white wine
115g/4oz asparagus spears or green
  beans, sliced and blanched
2 young carrots, sliced and blanched
50g/2oz/¾ cup button mushrooms
salt and ground black pepper
50g/2oz Parmesan or pecorino
  cheese, grated, to serve

--- COOK'S TIP ---

Pecorino, a sheep's milk cheese, is a good choice if allergic to cow's milk.

1 It is important to follow the steps for making real risotto so that you achieve the right texture. First heat the stock in a saucepan until simmering. Next to it, in a large saucepan, sauté the onion and garlic in the oil and butter for 3 minutes.

2 Stir the rice into the onion mixture, making sure each grain is coated well in the oil, then stir in the wine. Allow the wine to evaporate then spoon in two ladlefuls of hot stock, stirring continuously

3 Allow this to evaporate, then add more stock and stir again. Continue like this, ladling in the stock and stirring frequently for around 20 minutes, by which time the rice will have swelled greatly.

4 Mix in the asparagus or beans, carrots and mushrooms, season well, and cook for 1–2 minutes more. Serve immediately in bowls with a scattering of grated cheese.

Pistachio Pilaff

Saffron and ginger are traditional rice spices and delicious when mixed with fresh pistachios.

INGREDIENTS

Serves 4

3 onions
60ml/4 tbsp olive oil
2 garlic cloves, crushed
2.5cm/1in piece fresh root
  ginger, grated
1 green chilli, chopped
2 carrots, coarsely grated
225g/8oz/generous 1 cup basmati
  rice, rinsed
1.5ml/¼ tsp saffron strands, crushed
450ml/¾ pint/1⅞ cups stock
5cm/2in cinnamon stick
5ml/1 tsp ground coriander
salt and ground black pepper
75g/3oz/¼ cup fresh pistachios
450g/1lb fresh leaf spinach
5ml/1 tsp garam masala
tomato salad, to serve

1 Roughly chop two of the onions. Heat half the oil in a large saucepan and fry the onion with half the garlic, the ginger and the chilli for 5 minutes until softened.

2 Mix in the carrots and rice, cook for 1 more minute and then add the saffron, stock, cinnamon and coriander. Season well. Bring to the boil, then cover and simmer gently for 10 minutes without lifting the lid.

3 Remove from the heat and leave to stand, uncovered, for 5 minutes. Add the pistachios, mixing them in with a fork. Remove the cinnamon stick and keep the rice warm.

4 Thinly slice the third onion and fry in the remaining oil for about 3 minutes. Stir in the spinach. Cover and cook for another 2 minutes.

5 Add the garam masala powder. Cook until just tender, then drain and roughly chop the spinach.

6 Spoon the spinach round the edge of a round serving dish and pile the pilaff in the centre. Serve immediately with a tomato salad.

Coulibiac

This traditional Russian dish, made with fish and rice wrapped in dough, can be adapted to make a light, crisp vegetarian dish with filo pastry and green lentils.

INGREDIENTS

Serves 6

175g/6oz/1 cup green lentils,
  soaked for 30 minutes
1.2 litres/2 pints/5 cups stock
2 bay leaves
2 onions, sliced
175g/6oz/³/₄ cup butter, melted
225g/8oz/1 cup basmati rice
60ml/4 tbsp chopped fresh parsley
30ml/2 tbsp chopped fresh dill
1 egg, beaten
225g/8oz/3 cups mushrooms, sliced
about 8 sheets filo pastry
3 eggs, hard-boiled and sliced
salt and ground black pepper

1 Drain the lentils then simmer them in half the stock, with the bay leaves and one onion, for 25 minutes until cooked and thick. Season well and set aside to cool.

2 Gently fry the remaining onion in another saucepan with 30ml/2 tbsp of the butter for 5 minutes. Stir in the rice then the rest of the stock.

3 Season, bring to the boil, then cover and simmer for 12 minutes. Leave the rice to stand, uncovered, for 5 minutes then stir in the fresh herbs. Cool, then beat in the raw egg.

4 Fry the mushrooms in 45ml/3 tbsp of the butter for 5 minutes until they are just soft. Set aside to cool.

5 Brush the inside of a large, shallow ovenproof dish with more butter. Lay the sheets of filo in it, covering the base and with enough overhanging the sides to enclose the filling. Brush the layers with butter as you go.

6 Layer the rice, lentils and mushrooms in the pastry case, repeating the layers at least once and tucking the egg in-between. Season as you layer and form an even mound.

7 Bring up the sheets of pastry over the filling, scrunching the top into attractive folds. Brush the pie all over with the rest of the melted butter and put to one side to firm up.

8 Preheat the oven to 190°C/375°F/ Gas 5. When ready, bake the coulibiac for about 45 minutes until golden and crisp. Allow to stand for 10 minutes before you cut and serve.

Caribbean Coconut Rice

This is a great family favourite in West Indian culture. Serve with the gravy sauce, and slices of fried aubergine if you like.

INGREDIENTS

Serves 4

225g/8oz/generous 1 cup easy-cook
    long grain rice
115g/4oz/¼ cup dried gunga peas,
    soaked and cooked but still firm
750ml/1¼ pints/3 cups water
50g/2oz/¾ cup creamed
    coconut, chopped
15ml/1 tbsp chopped fresh thyme or
    5ml/1 tsp dried thyme
1 small onion, stuck with
    6 whole cloves
salt and ground black pepper

1 Put all the ingredients into a large saucepan with the salt and pepper.

2 Bring the mixture to the boil, stirring until the coconut melts, then cover and simmer for 20 minutes.

3 Remove the lid and cook uncovered for 5 minutes to evaporate any excess liquid. Remove from the heat and stir to separate the grains. The rice should be quite dry.

Lentils and Rice

The long grain Patna rice is a favourite in India for use in everyday cooking

INGREDIENTS

Serves 4–6

60ml/4 tbsp ghee or melted butter
1 onion, finely chopped
2 garlic cloves, crushed
2.5cm/1in piece fresh root
    ginger, shredded
4 green chillies, chopped
4 whole cloves
2.5cm/1in cinnamon stick
4 green cardamom pods
5ml/1 tsp ground turmeric
salt, to taste
325g/12oz/scant 1½ cups Patna rice,
    washed and soaked for 20 minutes
175g/6oz/¾ cups split green lentils,
    washed and soaked for 20 minutes
600ml/1 pint/2½ cups water

1 Gently heat the ghee or butter in a large heavy saucepan with a tight-fitting lid and fry the onion, garlic, ginger, chillies, and spices and salt until the onion is soft and translucent.

2 Drain the rice and lentils, add to the spice mixture and sauté for 2–3 minutes. Add the water and bring to the boil. Reduce the heat, cover, and cook for about 20–25 minutes or until all the water is absorbed.

3 Take the pan off the heat and leave to rest for 5 minutes. Just before serving, gently toss the mixture with a palette knife or large fork.

────── COOK'S TIP ──────

Frying the spices for a few minutes before adding the rice, lentils and water allows them to sweeten and become more aromatic.

Egg Foo Yung

A great way of turning a bowl of leftover cooked rice into a meal for four, this oriental dish is tasty and full of texture.

INGREDIENTS

Serves 4

3 eggs, beaten
pinch of five-spice powder (optional)
45ml/3 tbsp groundnut or
    sunflower oil
4 spring onions, sliced
1 garlic clove, crushed
1 small green pepper, seeded
    and chopped
115g/4oz fresh beansprouts
225g/8oz/3 cups cooked long
    grain rice
45ml/3 tbsp light soy sauce
15ml/1 tbsp sesame oil
salt and ground black pepper

1 Season the eggs and beat in the five-spice powder, if using. In a wok or large frying pan, heat one tablespoon of the oil and when quite hot, pour in the egg.

2 Cook the egg, lifting the mixture away from the sides and allowing the liquid to slip underneath, until the omelette is firm. Then tip out and slice into small strips.

3 Heat the remaining oil and stir-fry the onion, garlic, pepper and beansprouts for about 2 minutes, stirring and tossing continuously.

4 Mix in the cooked rice and heat thoroughly, stirring well. Add the soy sauce and sesame oil and adjust the seasoning if necessary. Add the omelette strips and mix in well. Serve piping hot.

Basmati and Nut Pilaff

Use whatever nuts are your favourite in this dish – even unsalted peanuts are good, although almonds, cashew nuts or pistachios are more exotic.

INGREDIENTS

Serves 4–6
225g/8oz/generous 1 cup basmati rice
1 onion, chopped
1 garlic clove, crushed
1 large carrot, coarsely grated
15–30ml/1–2 tbsp sunflower oil
5ml/1 tsp cumin seeds
10ml/2 tsp ground coriander
10ml/2 tsp black mustard seeds
  (optional)
4 green cardamom pods
450ml/³/₄ pint/1⁷/₈ cups stock or water
1 bay leaf
75g/3oz/¹/₂ cup unsalted nuts
salt and ground black pepper
fresh chopped parsley or coriander,
  to garnish

1 Wash the rice in a sieve under cold running water. If there is time, soak the rice for 30 minutes, then drain it well in a sieve.

2 In a large shallow frying pan, gently fry the onion, garlic and carrot in the oil for 3–4 minutes.

3 Stir in the rice and spices and cook for a further 1–2 minutes so that the grains are coated in oil.

4 Pour in the stock or water, add the bay leaf and season well. Bring to the boil, cover and simmer very gently.

5 Remove from the heat without lifting the lid. Leave to stand on one side for about 5 minutes.

6 If the rice is cooked, there will be small steam holes in the centre of the pan. Discard the bay leaf and the cardamom pods.

7 Stir in the nuts and check the seasoning. Scatter over the chopped parsley or coriander.

SIDE DISHES AND SNACKS

*Rice is not only for main meals. It lends
itself easily to quick light food and even
canapés. Japanese sushi is perhaps the
best-known quick rice meal – seasoned
sticky rice is shaped deftly into rolls or
moulds to be served with sliced fish or
wrapped in seaweed sheets. Creamy
risotto rice is obligingly easy to form
into bite-size balls when cold, ready for
coating in crumbs and deep frying,
whilst long grain rice can be rolled
inside vine leaves for the classic Greek
appetiser, Dolmades. Then there is the
other great use of rice – as a tasty
accompaniment to a colourful selection of
vegetables or flavourings.*

Spicy Rice Cakes

INGREDIENTS

Makes 16 cakes
1 garlic clove, crushed
1cm/½ in piece fresh root ginger,
    peeled and finely chopped
1.5ml/¼ tsp ground turmeric
5ml/1 tsp sugar
2.5ml/½ tsp salt
5ml/1 tsp chilli sauce
10ml/2 tsp fish or soy sauce
30ml/2 tbsp chopped fresh coriander
juice of ½ lime
115g/4oz/generous ½ cup dry weight
    long grain rice, cooked
peanuts, chopped
150ml/¼ pint/⅔ cup vegetable oil, for
    deep-frying
coriander sprigs, to garnish

1 In a food processor, process the garlic, ginger and turmeric. Add the sugar, salt, chilli and fish or soy sauce, coriander and lime juice.

2 Add three-quarters of the cooked rice and process until smooth and sticky. Transfer to a mixing bowl and stir in the remainder of the rice. Wet your hands and shape into thumb-size balls.

3 Roll the balls in chopped peanuts to coat evenly. Then set aside until ready to cook and serve.

4 Heat the vegetable oil in a deep frying pan. Prepare a tray lined with kitchen paper to drain the rice cakes. Deep-fry three cakes at a time until crisp and golden, remove with a slotted spoon, then drain on the kitchen paper before serving hot.

Red Rice Rissoles

INGREDIENTS

Serves 6
1 large red onion, chopped
1 red pepper, chopped
2 garlic cloves, crushed
1 red chilli, finely chopped
30ml/2 tbsp olive oil
25g/1oz/2 tbsp butter
225g/8oz/generous 1 cup risotto rice
1 litre/1¾ pints/4 cups stock
4 sun-dried tomatoes, chopped
30ml/2 tbsp tomato purée
10ml/2 tsp dried oregano
45ml/3 tbsp chopped fresh parsley
150g/6oz cheese, e.g. red Leicester or
    smoked Cheddar
1 egg, beaten
115g/4oz/1 cup dried breadcrumbs
oil, for deep frying
salt and ground black pepper

1 Fry the onion, pepper, garlic and chilli in the oil and butter for 5 minutes. Stir in the rice and fry for a further 2 minutes.

2 Pour in the stock and add the sun-dried tomatoes, purée, oregano and seasoning. Bring to the boil, stirring occasionally, then cover and simmer for 20 minutes.

3 Stir in the parsley then turn into a shallow dish and chill until firm. When cold, divide into 12 and shape into equally-sized balls.

4 Cut the cheese into 12 pieces and press a nugget into the centre of each rice rissole.

5 Put the beaten egg in one bowl and the breadcrumbs into another. Dip the rissoles first into the egg, then into the breadcrumbs, coating each of them evenly.

6 Place the rissoles on a plate and chill again for 30 minutes. Fill a deep frying pan one-third full of oil and heat until a cube of day-old bread browns in under a minute.

7 Fry the rissoles in batches for about 3–4 minutes, reheating the oil in-between. Drain on kitchen paper and keep warm, uncovered. Serve with a side salad.

Stuffed Peppers

INGREDIENTS

Serves 6

6 mixed peppers (red, yellow
  and green)
30ml/2 tbsp olive oil
1 large onion, finely chopped
3–4 spring onions, finely chopped
250g/9oz minced lamb
2 garlic cloves, crushed (optional)
50g/2oz/¼ cup yellow split peas
75g/3oz/½ cup cooked long grain rice
30ml/2 tbsp finely chopped
  fresh parsley
30ml/2 tbsp finely chopped fresh mint
30ml/2 tbsp finely snipped fresh chives
5ml/1 tsp ground cinnamon
juice of 2 lemons
30ml/2 tbsp tomato purée (optional)
400g/14oz can chopped tomatoes
knob of butter
salt and ground black pepper
natural yogurt and naan, to serve

1 Cut off the pepper tops and set aside. Remove the seeds and cores and trim the bases so they stand squarely. Cook in boiling salted water for 5 minutes, then drain, rinse under cold water and set aside.

2 Heat the oil in a large saucepan or flameproof casserole and fry the onion and spring onions for about 4–5 minutes until golden brown. Add the lamb and fry over a moderate heat until well browned, stirring frequently. Stir in the garlic, if using.

3 Place the split peas in a small pan with enough water to cover, bring to the boil and then simmer gently for 12–15 minutes until soft. Drain.

4 Stir the split peas, cooked rice, herbs, cinnamon, juice of one lemon, and the tomato purée, if using, into the meat. Season with salt and pepper and stir until well combined.

5 Spoon the rice and split pea mixture into the peppers and place the reserved lids on top.

6 Pour the chopped tomatoes into a large saucepan or flameproof casserole and add the remaining lemon juice and butter. Arrange the peppers in the pan with the stems upwards. Bring to the boil, then cover tightly and cook over a low heat for 40–45 minutes until the peppers are tender.

7 Serve the peppers with the tomato sauce, yogurt and naan.

Dolmades

Dolmeh, meaning "stuffed" in Persian, generally refers to any vegetable or fruit stuffed with meat, rice and herbs. It is a favourite dish throughout the Middle East.

INGREDIENTS

Serves 4–6
250g/9oz vine leaves
30ml/2 tbsp olive oil
1 large onion, finely chopped
250g/9oz minced lamb
50g/2oz/¼ cup yellow split peas
75g/3oz/½ cup cooked long grain rice
30ml/2 tbsp chopped fresh parsley
30ml/2 tbsp chopped fresh mint
30ml/2 tbsp snipped fresh chives
3–4 spring onions, finely chopped
juice of 2 lemons
30ml/2 tbsp tomato purée (optional)
30ml/2 tbsp sugar
salt and ground black pepper
natural yogurt and pitta bread, to serve

1 Blanch fresh vine leaves, if using, in boiling water for 1–2 minutes to soften them, or rinse preserved, bottled or canned vine leaves under cold water.

2 Heat the oil in a large frying pan and fry the onion for 3–4 minutes until slightly softened. Add the lamb and fry over a moderate heat until well browned, stirring frequently. Season with salt and pepper.

3 Place the split peas in a small pan with enough water to cover and bring to the boil. Cover the pan and simmer for 12–15 minutes until soft. Drain the split peas, if necessary.

4 Stir the split peas, cooked rice, chopped herbs, spring onions, and the juice of one of the lemons into the meat. Add the tomato purée, if using, and then knead the mixture with your hands until thoroughly blended.

5 Flatten out a vine leaf with the vein side up. Place 15ml/1 tbsp of the meat mixture on the leaf and fold the stem end over the meat. Fold the sides in towards the centre and then fold over to make a neat parcel. Continue until all the filling has been used up.

COOK'S TIP

If using preserved vine leaves, soak them overnight in cold water and rinse several times before use.

6 Line the base of a large saucepan with several unstuffed leaves and arrange the rolled leaves in tight layers on top. Stir the remaining lemon juice and the sugar into about 150ml/ ¼ pint/⅔ cup water and pour over the leaves. Place a small heat-resistant plate over the Dolmades to keep them in shape. Cover the pan with a tight-fitting lid and cook over a very low heat for 2 hours, checking occasionally and adding a little extra water if the pan begins to boil dry. Serve warm or cold with yogurt and warm pitta bread.

Basmati and Lentil Salad

INGREDIENTS

Serves 6

115g/4oz/1 cup Puy lentils
225g/8oz/generous 1 cup basmati rice,
  well rinsed
2 carrots, coarsely grated
1 cucumber, halved, seeded and
  coarsely grated
3 spring onions, sliced
45ml/3 tbsp chopped fresh parsley

For the dressing

30ml/2 tbsp sunflower oil
30ml/2 tbsp extra virgin olive oil
30ml/2 tbsp white wine vinegar
30ml/2 tbsp fresh lemon juice
generous pinch of granulated sugar
salt and ground black pepper

1 Soak the lentils for 30 minutes. Meanwhile, make the dressing by shaking all the ingredients together in a screw-top jar. Set aside.

2 Drain the lentils then boil them in unsalted water for 20–25 minutes or until soft. Drain thoroughly.

3 Meanwhile boil the basmati rice in lightly salted water for 10 minutes, then drain.

4 Mix together the rice and lentils in the dressing and season well. Leave to cool thoroughly.

5 Add the carrots, cucumber, onions and parsley. Spoon into a serving dish and chill before serving.

COOK'S TIP

Puy lentils from France are small, deliciously nutty pulses, highly prized by gourmets. They blend beautifully with aromatic basmati rice.

Wild Rice with Julienne Vegetables

INGREDIENTS

Serves 4

115g/4oz/1 cup wild rice, soaked
1 red onion, sliced
2 carrots, cut into julienne sticks
2 celery sticks, cut into julienne sticks
50g/2oz/4 tbsp butter
150ml/¼ pint/⅓ cup stock or water
2 courgettes, cut in thicker sticks
salt and ground black pepper
a few toasted almond flakes, to garnish

1 Drain the rice, then boil in unsalted water for 15–20 minutes, until it is soft and many of the grains have burst open. Drain well.

2 In another saucepan, gently fry the onion, carrots and celery in the butter for 2 minutes then pour in the stock or water and season well.

3 Bring to the boil, simmer for 2 minutes then stir in the courgettes. Cook for 1 more minute then mix in the rice. Reheat and serve hot garnished with the almonds.

Sushi

INGREDIENTS

Makes 8–10
Tuna sushi
3 sheets nori (paper-thin seaweed)
150g/5oz fresh tuna fillet, cut
  into fingers
5ml/1 tsp wasabi (Japanese horseradish)
6 young carrots, blanched
450g/1lb/6 cups cooked Japanese rice

Salmon sushi
2 eggs
2.5ml/½ tsp salt
10ml/2 tsp sugar
5 sheets nori
450g/1lb/6 cups cooked Japanese rice
150g/5oz fresh salmon fillet, cut
  into fingers
5ml/1 tsp wasabi paste
½ small cucumber, cut into strips

1 To make the tuna sushi, spread half a sheet of nori on to a bamboo mat, lay strips of tuna across the full length and season with the thinned wasabi. Place a line of blanched carrot next to the tuna and roll tightly. Moisten the edge with water and seal.

2 Place a square of damp wax paper on to the bamboo mat, then spread evenly with sushi rice. Place the non-wrapped tuna along the centre and wrap tightly, enclosing the nori completely. Remove the paper and cut into neat rounds with a wet knife.

3 To make the salmon sushi, make a simple flat omelette by beating together the eggs, salt and sugar. Heat a large non-stick pan, pour in the egg mixture, stir briefly and allow to set. Transfer to a clean dish towel and cool.

4 Place the nori on to a bamboo mat, cover with the omelette, and trim to size. Spread a layer of rice over the omelette, then lay strips of salmon across the width. Season the salmon with the thinned wasabi, then place a strip of cucumber next to the salmon. Fold the bamboo mat in half. Cut into neat rounds with a wet knife.

Fried Rice Balls

These deep fried balls of risotto are stuffed with mozzarella cheese. They are very popular snacks in Rome and central Italy.

INGREDIENTS

Serves 4
1 quantity cooked risotto
3 eggs
115g/4oz/1 cup mozzarella cheese,
  cut into small dice
oil, for deep-frying
breadcrumbs, as required
flour, to coat

1 Allow the risotto to cool completely. (The balls are better when formed from risotto made the day before.) Beat two of the eggs, and mix them into the cold risotto.

2 Use your hands to form the rice mixture into balls the size of a large egg. If the mixture is too moist to hold its shape well, stir in a few tablespoons of the breadcrumbs. Poke a hole into the centre of each ball, fill it with a few cubes of mozzarella, and close the hole again with the rice mixture.

3 Heat the oil until a small piece of bread sizzles as soon as it is dropped in (about 185°C/360°F).

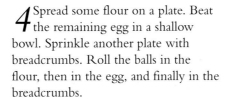

4 Spread some flour on a plate. Beat the remaining egg in a shallow bowl. Sprinkle another plate with breadcrumbs. Roll the balls in the flour, then in the egg, and finally in the breadcrumbs.

5 Fry the rice balls a few at a time in the hot oil until golden and crisp. Drain on kitchen paper while the remaining balls are frying. Serve hot.

Indonesian Coconut Rice

This is a very popular way of cooking rice throughout the whole of South-east Asia, and goes particularly well with fish, chicken and pork.

INGREDIENTS

Serves 4–6

350g/12oz/scant 1½ cups Thai fragrant rice
400ml/14fl oz can coconut milk
300ml/½ pint/1¼ cups water
2.5ml/½ tsp ground coriander
5cm/2in cinnamon stick
1 lemon grass stalk, bruised
1 bay leaf (optional)
salt
deep-fried onions, to garnish

1 Wash the rice in several changes of water and then put in a pan with the coconut milk, water, coriander, cinnamon stick, lemon grass, bay leaf, if using, and salt. Bring to the boil, stirring to prevent the rice from setting on the base of the pan. Cover and cook over a low heat for 12–15 minutes, or until all the liquid has been absorbed.

2 Fork the rice through carefully and remove the cinnamon stick, lemon grass and bay leaf. Cover the pan with a tight-fitting lid and then cook gently over the lowest possible heat for a further 3–5 minutes.

3 Pile the rice onto a warm serving dish and serve garnished with the crisp deep-fried onions.

Spinach and Rice

A thick layer of spinach makes a lovely topping for this rice dish.

INGREDIENTS

Serves 4

40g/1½oz/3 tbsp butter or margarine
1 onion, finely chopped
2 tomatoes, chopped
450g/1lb/generous 2¼ cups basmati rice, washed
2 garlic cloves, crushed
600ml/1 pint/2½ cups stock or water
350g/12oz fresh spinach, shredded
salt and ground black pepper
2 tomatoes, sliced, to garnish

1 Melt 25g/1oz/2 tbsp of the butter or margarine in a large saucepan and fry the onion for a few minutes until soft. Stir in the tomatoes.

2 Add the rice and garlic, cook for 5 minutes, then gradually add the stock, stirring all the time. Season well.

3 Cover the pan and simmer the rice for 10–15 minutes until it is almost cooked, then reduce the heat to low.

4 Spread the spinach in a thick layer over the rice. Cover the pan and cook over a low heat for 5–8 minutes until the spinach has wilted. Dot the remaining butter over the top and then serve, garnished with sliced tomatoes.

Lemon and Herb Risotto Cake

This unusual rice dish can also be served as a main course with salad. It is good served cold, and packs well for picnics.

INGREDIENTS

Serves 4
1 small leek, thinly sliced
600ml/1 pint/2½ cups chicken stock
225g/8oz/generous 1 cup risotto or
  short grain pudding rice
finely grated rind of 1 lemon
30ml/2 tbsp snipped fresh chives
30ml/2 tbsp chopped fresh parsley
75g/3oz/¼ cup grated
  mozzarella cheese
salt and ground black pepper
parsley sprigs and lemon wedges,
  to garnish

1 Preheat the oven to 200°C/400°F/ Gas 6. Lightly oil a 22cm/8½ in round, loose-based cake tin.

2 Cook the leek in a large saucepan with 45ml/3 tbsp stock, stirring over a moderate heat, to soften. Add the rice and the remaining stock.

3 Bring to the boil. Cover the pan and simmer gently, stirring occasionally, for about 20 minutes, or until all the liquid is absorbed.

4 Stir in the lemon rind, herbs, cheese and seasoning. Spoon into the tin, cover with foil and bake for 30–35 minutes or until lightly browned. Turn out and serve in slices, garnished with parsley sprigs and lemon wedges.

--- COOK'S TIP ---

Lightly simmering vegetables in stock instead of sautéeing in oil or butter helps to cut down on fat.

Saffron Rice with Cardamoms

Aromatic green cardamom pods, cloves and saffron give this dish a delicate flavour and colour.

INGREDIENTS

Serves 6

450g/1lb/generous 2¼ cups
  basmati rice
750ml/1¼ pints/3 cups water
3 green cardamom pods
2 cloves
5ml/1 tsp salt
2.5ml/½ tsp crushed saffron strands
45ml/3 tbsp semi-skimmed milk

1 Wash and drain the rice at least twice and place it in a large saucepan with the water.

2 Toss the whole spices into the saucepan along with the salt. Bring to the boil, cover and simmer gently for about 10 minutes.

3 Test the rice and, when cooked, drain it through a sieve. Meanwhile, place the saffron and milk in a small saucepan and heat it gently. Alternatively, put the ingredients in a cup and warm them together for 1 minute in the microwave.

4 Put the rice back into its pan and pour the saffron milk over the top. Cover with a tight-fitting lid and cook over a medium heat for 7–10 minutes.

5 Remove the saucepan from the heat and leave the rice to stand for 5 minutes before serving.

Rice with Dill and Broad Beans

This is a favourite rice dish in Iran where it is called Baghali Polo.

INGREDIENTS

Serves 4
275g/10oz/scant 1½ cups basmati rice, soaked in salted water for 3 hours
45ml/3 tbsp melted butter
175g/6oz/1½ cups broad beans, fresh or frozen
90ml/6 tbsp finely chopped fresh dill
5ml/1 tsp ground cinnamon
5ml/1 tsp ground cumin
2–3 saffron strands, soaked in 15ml/ 1 tbsp boiling water
salt

1 Drain the rice and then boil it in fresh salted water for 5 minutes. Reduce the heat and simmer very gently for 10 minutes, until half-cooked. Drain and rinse in warm water.

2 Put 15ml/1 tbsp of the butter in a non-stick saucepan and add enough rice to cover the base. Add a quarter of the beans and a little dill.

3 Add another layer of rice, then a layer of beans and dill and continue layering until all the beans and dill are used up, finishing with a layer of rice. Cook over a gentle heat for 10 minutes.

4 Pour the remaining melted butter over the rice. Sprinkle with the cinnamon and cumin. Cover the pan with a clean dish towel and secure with a tight-fitting lid, lifting the corners of the cloth back over the lid. Steam over a low heat for 30–45 minutes.

5 Mix 45ml/3 tbsp of the rice with the saffron water. Spoon the remaining rice onto a large serving plate and scatter on the saffron-flavoured rice to decorate. Serve with either a lamb or chicken dish.

COOK'S TIP

Saffron may seem expensive, however you only need a little to add flavour and colour to a variety of savoury and sweet dishes. And, as long as it is kept dry and dark, it never goes off.

Sweet and Sour Rice

This popular Middle Eastern dish is flavoured with fruit and spices and is commonly served with chicken.

INGREDIENTS

Serves 4
50g/2oz *zereshk*
45ml/3 tbsp melted butter
50g/2oz/¼ cup raisins
30ml/2 tbsp sugar
5ml/1 tsp ground cinnamon
5ml/1 tsp ground cumin
350g/12oz/scant 1½ cups basmati rice,
　soaked in salted water for 2 hours
2–3 saffron strands, soaked in 15ml/
　1 tbsp boiling water
pinch of salt

1 Thoroughly wash the *zereshk* in cold water at least 4–5 times to rinse off any bits of grit.

2 Heat 15ml/1 tbsp of the butter in a small frying pan and stir-fry the raisins for 1–2 minutes.

3 Add the *zereshk*, fry for a few seconds, and then add the sugar, and half of the cinnamon and cumin. Cook briefly and then set aside.

4 Drain the rice, then boil in salted water for 5 minutes. Reduce the heat and simmer for 10 minutes until the rice is half-cooked.

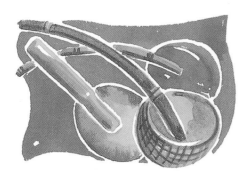

5 Drain and rinse the rice well in warm water and wash and dry the pan. Heat half the remaining butter in the pan, add 15ml/1 tbsp water and stir in half of the cooked rice. Sprinkle with half of the raisin and *zereshk* mixture and top with all but 45ml/ 3 tbsp of the rice. Sprinkle over the remaining raisin mixture.

6 Blend the reserved rice with the remaining cinnamon and cumin and scatter over the rice mixture. Dribble the remaining butter over then cover the pan with a clean dish towel and secure with a tight-fitting lid, lifting the corners of the cloth back over the lid. Steam the rice over a very low heat for about 30–40 minutes.

7 Just before serving, mix 45ml/ 3 tbsp of the rice with the saffron water. Spoon the rice onto a large flat serving dish and scatter the saffron rice over the top to decorate.

Thai Rice

This is a lovely, soft, fluffy rice dish, perfumed with fresh lemon grass and limes.

INGREDIENTS

Serves 4

1 lemon grass stalk
2 limes
225g/8oz/generous 1 cup brown
  basmati rice
15ml/1 tbsp olive oil
1 onion, chopped
2.5cm/1in piece fresh root ginger,
  peeled and finely chopped
7.5ml/1½ tsp coriander seeds
7.5ml/1½ tsp cumin seeds
750ml/1¼ pints/3 cups vegetable stock
60ml/4 tbsp chopped fresh coriander
lime wedges, to serve

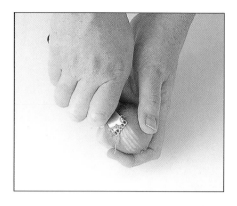

1 Finely chop the lemon grass. Then remove the zest from the limes using a zester or a fine grater.

2 Rinse the rice in plenty of cold water until the water runs clear. Drain through a sieve.

3 Heat the oil in a large pan and add the onion, spices, lemon grass and lime zest and cook for 2–3 minutes.

4 Add the drained rice and cook for 1 minute, then add the stock and bring to the boil. Reduce the heat to very low and cover the pan. Cook gently for 30 minutes then check the rice. If it is still crunchy, cover the pan and leave for a further 3–5 minutes. Remove from the heat.

5 Stir in the fresh coriander, fluff up the grains, cover and leave for 10 minutes. Serve with lime wedges.

Rice and Peas

This sweet and spicy dish has its origins in the Caribbean, where coconut is a popular ingredient in savoury dishes.

INGREDIENTS

Serves 6

175g/6oz/1 cup dried red kidney beans
2 fresh thyme sprigs
50g/2oz creamed coconut
2 bay leaves
1 onion, finely chopped
2 garlic cloves, crushed
2.5ml/½ tsp ground allspice
115g/4oz chopped red or green pepper
450g/1lb/generous 2¼ cups long
  grain rice
salt and ground black pepper

1 Place the red kidney beans in a large bowl. Cover with water and leave to soak overnight.

COOK'S TIP

Dried red kidney beans must be initially boiled vigorously for 15 minutes before lowering the heat and cooking them until tender. This ensures that natural toxins present in the beans are eliminated.

2 Drain the beans, place in a large pan and add enough water to cover by about 2.5cm/1in. Bring to the boil and boil vigorously over a high heat for 15 minutes, drain, add fresh water, and simmer for about 1½ hours or until the beans are tender.

3 Add the thyme, creamed coconut, bay leaves, onion, garlic, allspice, red or green pepper and seasoning and stir in 600ml/1 pint/2½ cups water.

4 Bring to the boil and add the rice. Stir well, reduce the heat and simmer, covered, for 25–30 minutes, until all the liquid is absorbed. Serve as an accompaniment to fish, meat or vegetarian dishes.

Tomato Rice

This delicious dish can also be served as a popular vegetarian main course.

INGREDIENTS

Serves 4
30ml/2 tbsp corn oil
2.5ml/½ tsp onion seeds
1 onion, sliced
2 tomatoes, sliced
1 orange or yellow pepper, sliced
5ml/1 tsp ginger pulp
5ml/1 tsp garlic pulp
5ml/1 tsp chilli powder
30ml/2 tbsp chopped fresh coriander
1 potato, diced
7.5ml/1½ tsp salt
50g/2oz/½ cup frozen peas
400g/14oz/2 cups basmati rice, washed
750ml/1¼ pints/3 cups water

1 Heat the oil and fry the onion seeds for about 30 seconds. Add the sliced onion and fry for about 5 minutes.

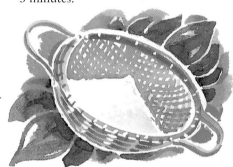

2 Gradually add the sliced tomatoes, pepper, ginger, garlic, chilli powder, fresh coriander, potato, salt and peas and stir-fry over a medium heat for a further 5 minutes.

3 Add the rice and stir for about 1 minute until well coated.

4 Pour in the water and bring the rice to the boil, then lower the heat to medium. Cover and cook for 12–15 minutes. Leave the rice to stand for 5 minutes and then serve.

Pea and Mushroom Pilau

It is best to use button mushrooms and petit pois for this delectable rice dish.

INGREDIENTS

Serves 6
450g/1lb/2¼ cups basmati rice
30ml/2 tbsp vegetable oil
2.5ml/½ tsp black cumin seeds
2 black cardamom pods
2.5cm/2in cinnamon sticks
3 garlic cloves, sliced
5ml/1 tsp salt
1 tomato, sliced
50g/2oz/¾ cup button mushrooms
75g/3oz/1 cup petit pois
750ml/1¼ pints/3 cups water

1 Wash the rice at least twice and set aside in a sieve to drain thoroughly.

2 In a medium saucepan, heat the oil and add the spices, garlic and salt.

3 Add the sliced tomato and button mushrooms and stir-fry the mixture for 2–3 minutes.

4 Add the drained rice and peas and stir gently, making sure you do not break the rice.

5 Add the water and bring to the boil. Lower the heat, cover and continue to cook for 15–20 minutes.

Tanzanian Vegetable Rice

Serve this tasty dish with baked chicken or fish. Add the vegetables near the end of cooking so that they remain crisp.

INGREDIENTS

Serves 4

350g/12oz/scant 1½ cups basmati rice
45ml/3 tbsp vegetable oil
1 onion, chopped
2 garlic cloves, crushed
750ml/1¼ pints/3 cups vegetable stock
  or water
115g/4oz/1 cup sweetcorn
½ red or green pepper, chopped
1 large carrot, grated

1 Wash the rice in a sieve under cold water, then leave to drain thoroughly for about 15 minutes.

2 Heat the oil in a large saucepan and fry the onion for a few minutes over a moderate heat until it just becomes soft.

3 Add the rice and stir-fry for about 10 minutes, taking care to keep stirring all the time so that the rice doesn't stick to the pan.

4 Add the garlic and the stock or water and stir well. Bring to the boil and cook over a high heat for 5 minutes, then reduce the heat, cover and cook for 20 minutes.

5 Scatter the sweetcorn over the rice, then spread the pepper on top and sprinkle over the grated carrot.

6 Cover the saucepan tightly and steam over a low heat until the rice is cooked, then mix together with a fork and serve immediately.

Rice with Seeds and Spices

This dish provides a change from plain boiled rice, and is a colourful accompaniment to serve with curries or grilled meats.

INGREDIENTS

Serves 4

5ml/1 tsp sunflower oil
2.5ml/½ tsp ground turmeric
6 green cardamom pods,
  lightly crushed
5ml/1 tsp coriander seeds,
  lightly crushed
1 garlic clove, crushed
200g/7oz/1 cup basmati rice
400ml/14fl oz/1⅔ cups stock
115g/4oz/½ cup natural yogurt
15ml/1 tbsp toasted sunflower seeds
15ml/1 tbsp toasted sesame seeds
salt and ground black pepper
coriander leaves, to garnish

1 Heat the oil in a non-stick frying pan and fry the spices and garlic for 1 minute, stirring all the time.

2 Add the rice and stock, bring to the boil, then cover and simmer for 15 minutes or until just tender.

3 Stir in the yogurt and the toasted sunflower and sesame seeds. Adjust the seasoning and serve the rice hot, garnished with coriander leaves.

Indian Pilau Rice

INGREDIENTS

Serves 4

225g/8oz/generous 1 cup basmati
 rice, rinsed well
30ml/2 tbsp vegetable oil
1 small onion, finely chopped
1 garlic clove, crushed
5ml/1 tsp fennel seeds
15ml/1 tbsp sesame seeds
2.5ml/$^{1}/_{2}$ tsp ground turmeric
5ml/1 tsp ground cumin
1.5ml/$^{1}/_{2}$ tsp salt
2 whole cloves
4 green cardamom pods,
 lightly crushed
5 black peppercorns
450ml/$^{3}/_{4}$ pint/1$^{7}/_{8}$ cups vegetable stock
15ml/1 tbsp ground almonds
coriander sprigs, to garnish

1 Soak the rice in water for 30 minutes. Heat the oil in a saucepan, add the onion and garlic, and fry gently for 5–6 minutes, until softened.

2 Stir in the fennel and sesame seeds, the turmeric, cumin, salt, cloves, cardamom pods and peppercorns and fry for about 1 minute. Drain the rice well, add it to the pan and stir-fry for a further 3 minutes.

3 Pour in the vegetable stock. Bring to the boil, then cover, reduce the heat to very low and simmer gently for 20 minutes, without removing the lid, until all the liquid has been absorbed.

4 Remove from the heat and leave to stand for 2–3 minutes. Fork up the rice and stir in the ground almonds. Garnish the rice with coriander sprigs.

Okra Fried Rice

Sliced okra provides a wonderful creamy texture to this delicious, simple dish.

INGREDIENTS

Serves 3–4

30ml/2 tbsp vegetable oil
15ml/1 tbsp butter or margarine
1 garlic clove, crushed
$^{1}/_{2}$ red onion, finely chopped
115g/4oz okra, topped and tailed
30ml/2 tbsp diced green and
 red peppers
2.5ml/$^{1}/_{2}$ tsp dried thyme
2 green chillies, finely chopped
2.5ml/$^{1}/_{2}$ tsp five-spice powder
1 vegetable stock cube
30ml/2 tbsp soy sauce
15ml/1 tbsp chopped fresh coriander
225g/8oz/3 cups cooked rice
salt and ground black pepper
coriander sprigs, to garnish

1 Heat the oil and the butter or margarine in a frying pan, add the garlic and onion and cook on a medium heat for 5 minutes until soft.

2 Thinly slice the okra, add to the frying pan and stir-fry gently for a further 6–7 minutes.

3 Add the green and red peppers, thyme, chillies and five-spice powder and cook for 3 minutes, then crumble in the stock cube.

4 Add the soy sauce, coriander and rice and heat through, stirring. Season with salt and pepper. Serve hot, garnished with coriander sprigs.

Joloff Rice

This is a good, basic flavoured rice that would go with any meat, poultry or fish dish.

INGREDIENTS

Serves 4

30ml/2 tbsp vegetable oil
1 large onion, chopped
2 garlic cloves, crushed
30ml/2 tbsp tomato purée
350g/12oz/scant 1³/₄ cups long
  grain rice
1 green chilli, seeded and chopped
pinch of salt
600ml/1 pint/2½ cups vegetable stock

1 Heat the oil in a large saucepan and fry the onion and garlic for 4–5 minutes until soft. Add the tomato purée and fry over a moderate heat for about 3 minutes, stirring all the time.

2 Rinse the rice in cold water, drain well and add to the pan with the chilli and the salt. Continue cooking for 2–3 minutes, stirring all the time to prevent the rice sticking to the pan.

3 Add the stock, bring to the boil, then cover and simmer over a low heat for about 15 minutes.

4 When the liquid is nearly absorbed, cover the rice with a piece of foil, cover the pan and steam, over a low heat, until the rice is thoroughly cooked.

COOK'S TIP

Always wash your hands straight after seeding and cutting chillies. If you have any cuts on your hands, prevent stinging by wearing rubber gloves while you chop.

Savoury Ground Rice

Savoury ground rice is served as an accompaniment to soups and stews in West Africa.

INGREDIENTS

Serves 4
300ml/¹/₂ pint/1¹/₄ cups milk
300ml/¹/₂ pint/1¹/₄ cups water
25g/1oz/2 tbsp butter or margarine
2.5ml/¹/₂ tsp salt
15ml/1 tbsp chopped fresh parsley
275g/10oz/1¹/₄ cups ground rice

1 Place the milk, water and butter or margarine in a saucepan, bring to the boil and add the salt and parsley.

2 Add the ground rice, stirring vigorously with a wooden spoon to prevent the rice becoming lumpy.

3 Cover the pan and cook over a low heat for about 15 minutes, beating the mixture every 2 minutes to prevent lumps forming.

4 To test if the rice is cooked, rub a pinch of the mixture between your fingers: if it feels smooth and fairly dry, it is ready. Serve hot.

___ COOK'S TIP ___

Ground rice is creamy white and when cooked has a slightly grainy texture. Although often used in sweet dishes, it is a tasty grain to serve with savoury dishes too. The addition of milk makes it creamier, but it can be omitted if preferred.

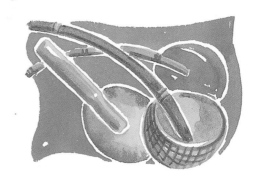

Sweet Rice

In Iran, sweet rice is always served at wedding banquets and on other traditional special occasions.

INGREDIENTS

Serves 8–10
3 oranges
90ml/6 tbsp sugar
45ml/3 tbsp melted butter
5–6 carrots, cut into julienne strips
50g/2oz/½ cup mixed chopped
  pistachios, almonds and pine nuts
675g/1½lb/3½ cups basmati rice,
  soaked in salted water for 2 hours
2–3 saffron strands, soaked in 15ml/
  1 tbsp boiling water
salt, to taste

1 Cut the peel from the oranges in wide strips using a potato peeler then cut the peel into thin shreds. Place in a saucepan with enough water to cover and bring to the boil. Simmer for a few minutes, drain and repeat until the peel is no longer bitter.

2 Place the peel back in the pan with 45ml/3 tbsp of the sugar and 60ml/4 tbsp water. Bring to the boil then simmer until the water is reduced by half. Set aside until needed.

3 Heat 15ml/1 tbsp of the butter in a pan and fry the carrots for 2–3 minutes. Add the remaining sugar and 60ml/4 tbsp water and simmer for 10 minutes until almost evaporated.

4 Stir the carrots and half of the nuts into the orange peel and set aside. Drain the rice, boil in salted water for 5 minutes, then reduce the heat and simmer very gently for 10 minutes until half-cooked. Drain and rinse.

5 Heat 15ml/1 tbsp of the remaining butter in the pan, add 45ml/3 tbsp water. Fork a little of the rice into the pan and spoon on some of the carrot mixture. Make layers until all the mixture has been used up.

6 Cook gently for 10 minutes. Pour over the remaining butter and cover the pan with a clean dish towel. Cover and steam for 30–45 minutes. Serve, garnished with the remaining nuts and the saffron water.

Rice and Fresh Herbs

You can choose your fresh herbs for this dish according to the main course it will accompany.

INGREDIENTS

Serves 4
350g/12oz/scant 1½ cups basmati rice,
  soaked in salt water for 2 hours
30ml/2 tbsp finely chopped
  fresh parsley
30ml/2 tbsp finely chopped
  fresh coriander
30ml/2 tbsp finely snipped fresh chives
15ml/1 tbsp finely chopped fresh dill
3–4 spring onions, finely chopped
60ml/4 tbsp butter
5ml/1 tsp ground cinnamon
2–3 saffron strands, soaked in 15ml/
  1 tbsp boiling water
pinch of salt

1 Drain the rice, and then boil in salted water for 5 minutes. Reduce the heat and simmer for 10 minutes.

2 Stir in the parsley, coriander, chives, dill and spring onions and mix well with a fork. Simmer for a few minutes more, then drain but do not rinse. Wash and dry the pan.

3 Heat half of the butter in the pan, add 15ml/1 tbsp water, then stir in the rice. Cook over a very low heat for 10 minutes, until half-cooked. Add the remaining butter, the cinnamon and saffron water and cover the pan with a clean dish towel. Secure with a tight-fitting lid, and steam over a very low heat for 30–40 minutes until tender.

Thai Rice with Bean Sprouts

Thai rice has a delicate fragrance that is delicious hot or cold.

INGREDIENTS

Serves 6

225g/8oz/1 cup Thai fragrant rice
30ml/2 tbsp sesame oil
30ml/2 tbsp fresh lime juice
1 small red chilli, seeded and chopped
1 garlic clove, crushed
10ml/2 tsp grated fresh root ginger
30ml/2 tbsp light soy sauce
5ml/1 tsp clear honey
45ml/3 tbsp pineapple juice
15ml/1 tbsp wine vinegar
2 spring onions, sliced
2 canned pineapple rings, chopped
150g/5oz/1¼ cups sprouted lentils or beansprouts
1 small red pepper, sliced
1 stick celery, sliced
50g/2oz/½ cup cashew nuts, chopped
30ml/2 tbsp toasted sesame seeds
salt and ground black pepper

1 Soak the Thai fragrant rice for 20 minutes, then rinse in several changes of water. Drain, then boil in salted water for 10–12 minutes until tender. Drain and set aside.

2 Whisk together the sesame oil, lime juice, chilli, garlic, ginger, soy sauce, honey, pineapple juice and wine vinegar in a large bowl. Stir in the rice.

3 Add the spring onions, pineapple rings, sprouted lentils or beansprouts, red pepper, celery, cashew nuts and the toasted sesame seeds and mix well. If the rice grains stick together on cooling, simply stir them with a metal spoon. This dish can be served warm or lightly chilled and is a good accompaniment to grilled or barbecued meats and fish.

COOK'S TIP

Sesame oil has a strong, nutty flavour and is used for seasoning, marinating or flavouring rather than for cooking. Because the taste is so distinctive, sesame oil can be mixed with grapeseed or other light-flavoured oils.

Rice Pilaff

This simple pilaff will complement most main course dishes. Alter the dried and fresh herbs to suit your meal.

INGREDIENTS

Serves 6–8

40g/1½oz/3 tbsp butter or
    45–60ml/3–4 tbsp oil
1 onion, finely chopped
450g/1lb/generous 2¼ cups long
    grain rice
750ml/1¼ pints/3 cups vegetable stock
    or water
2.5ml/½ tsp dried thyme
1 small bay leaf
salt and ground black pepper
15–30ml/1–2 tbsp chopped fresh
    parsley, dill or snipped chives,
    to garnish

1 In a large heavy saucepan, melt the butter or heat the oil over a medium heat. Add the onion and cook for 2–3 minutes until just softened, stirring all the time.

2 Add the rice and cook for 1–2 minutes until the rice becomes translucent, stirring frequently. Do not allow to brown.

3 Add the stock or water, dried thyme and bay leaf and season with salt and pepper. Bring to the boil over a high heat, stirring frequently. Just as the rice begins to boil, cover the surface with a round of foil and put the lid on the saucepan. Reduce the heat to very low and cook for 20 minutes (do not lift the cover or stir). Serve hot, garnished with fresh herbs.

— COOK'S TIP —

Once cooked the rice will remain hot for about half an hour, if tightly covered. To reheat the rice, spoon it into a microwave-safe bowl, cover with pierced clear film and microwave on full power for about 5 minutes until hot.

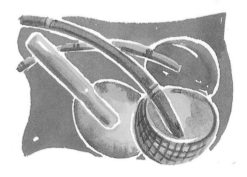

PUDDINGS

Every culture and cuisine seems to have at least one favourite dessert using rice. Even the cold northern Scandinavian countries have a popular winter rice pudding sprinkled liberally with warming cinnamon. In the more exotic climes of South-east Asia, glutinous sticky rices are simmered with sugar and served with coconut and lemon grass. Short grain pudding rices, flaked rice and ground rice are the more common favourites, but for an imaginative touch try using fragrant grains such as basmati or Thai Jasmine in the same way. Rice desserts come in many shapes, too, as they are easy to mould and can be transformed by adding whisked egg whites to them.

Thai Rice Cake

This celebration gâteau is made from fragrant Thai rice, tangy cream icing and fresh fruit.

INGREDIENTS

Serves 8–10

225g/8oz/1 cup Thai fragrant rice
1 litre/1³⁄₄ pints/4 cups milk
115g/4oz/¹⁄₂ cup caster sugar
6 green cardamom pods, crushed
2 bay leaves
300ml/¹⁄₂ pint/1¹⁄₄ cups
   whipping cream
6 eggs, separated

For the topping

300ml/¹⁄₂ pint/1¹⁄₄ cups double cream
200g/7oz quark
5ml/1 tsp vanilla essence
grated rind of 1 lemon
40g/1¹⁄₂ oz/3 tbsp caster sugar
soft berry fruits and sliced star or kiwi
   fruit, to decorate

1 Grease and line a 25cm/10in round deep cake tin. Boil the rice in unsalted water for 3 minutes and drain.

2 Return the rice to the pan with the milk, sugar, cardamoms and bay leaves. Bring to the boil, then lower the heat and simmer the rice for 20 minutes, stirring occasionally.

3 Allow the mixture to cool, then remove the bay leaves and any cardamom husks. Turn the mixture into a bowl. Beat in the cream and then the egg yolks. Preheat the oven to 180°C/350°F/Gas 4.

4 Whisk the egg whites until they form soft peaks, then fold them into the rice mixture. Spoon into the prepared tin and bake for 45–50 minutes until risen and golden brown. The centre should be slightly wobbly – it will firm up as the cake cools.

5 Chill the cake overnight in the tin. Turn it out onto a large serving plate. Whip the double cream until stiff then gently fold in the quark, vanilla essence, lemon rind and sugar.

6 Cover the top and sides of the cake with the cream mixture, swirling it attractively. Decorate with soft berry fruits and sliced star or kiwi fruit.

Rice Condé Sundae

Cook rice pudding on top of the hob instead of in the oven for a light, creamy texture. It is particularly good served cold topped with fruit, toasted nuts or a trickle of hot chocolate sauce.

INGREDIENTS

Serves 4

50g/2oz/generous ¼ cup short grain
   pudding rice
600ml/1 pint/2½ cups milk
5ml/1 tsp vanilla essence
2.5ml/½ tsp ground cinnamon
40g/1½ oz/3 tbsp granulated sugar

For the toppings
soft berry fruits such as strawberries,
   raspberries or blueberries
chocolate sauce and flaked toasted
   almonds (optional)

1 Place the rice, milk, vanilla essence, cinnamon and sugar in a saucepan. Bring to the boil, stirring constantly, then reduce the heat to a low simmer.

2 Cook the rice for 30–40 minutes, stirring occasionally. Add some extra milk if it begins to dry out.

3 Make sure the grains are soft, then remove the pan from the heat and allow the rice to cool, stirring it occasionally. When cold, chill the rice pudding in the fridge.

4 Before serving, stir the rice pudding and spoon it into four sundae dishes. Top with fresh fruits, chocolate sauce and almonds if using.

Ground Rice Pudding

This delicious and light ground rice pudding provides the perfect end to a spicy meal. It can be served hot or cold.

Ingredients

Serves 4–6
50g/2oz/¼ cup ground rice
25g/1oz/2 tbsp ground almonds
4 green cardamom pods, crushed
900ml/1½ pints/3¾ cups
   semi-skimmed milk
90ml/6 tbsp sugar
15ml/1 tbsp rose water

To garnish
15ml/1 tbsp crushed pistachios
silver leaf (optional)

1 Place the ground rice and almonds in a saucepan with the cardamom pods. Add 600ml/1 pint/2½ cups milk and bring to the boil over a medium heat, stirring occasionally.

2 Add the remaining milk and cook over a medium heat for about 10 minutes or until it thickens to the consistency of a creamy soup.

3 Stir in the sugar and rose water and continue cooking for a further 2 minutes. Serve garnished with pistachio nuts and silver leaf, if using.

Orange Rice Pudding

In Spain, Greece, Italy and Morocco, rice puddings are a favourite dish, especially when sweetened with honey and flavoured with orange.

Ingredients

Serves 4
50g/2oz/4 tbsp short grain
   pudding rice
600ml/1 pint/2½ cups milk
30–45ml/2–3 tbsp clear honey
finely grated rind of ½ small orange
150ml/¼ pint/⅔ cup double cream
15ml/1 tbsp chopped
   pistachios, toasted

1 Mix the rice with the milk, honey and orange rind in a saucepan.

2 Bring to the boil, then reduce the heat, cover and simmer very gently for about 1¼ hours, stirring regularly.

3 Remove the lid and continue cooking and stirring for about 15–20 minutes, until the rice is creamy.

4 Pour in the cream and simmer for 5–8 minutes longer. Serve the rice sprinkled with the pistachios in individual warmed bowls.

Fruited Rice Ring

This unusual rice pudding looks beautiful turned out of a ring mould but, if you prefer, stir the fruit into the rice and serve in individual dishes.

INGREDIENTS

Serves 4

65g/2½oz/5 tbsp short grain
   pudding rice
900ml/1½ pints/3¾ cups
   semi-skimmed milk
5cm/2½in cinnamon stick
175g/6oz/1½ cups dried fruit salad
175ml/6fl oz/¾ cup orange juice
45ml/3 tbsp caster sugar
finely grated rind of 1 small orange

1 Place the rice, milk and cinnamon stick in a large pan and bring to the boil. Cover and simmer, stirring occasionally, for about 1½ hours, until all the liquid has been absorbed.

2 Meanwhile, place the dried fruit salad and orange juice in a pan and bring to the boil. Cover and simmer very gently for about 1 hour, until the fruit is tender and no liquid remains.

3 Remove the cinnamon stick from the rice and gently stir in the caster sugar and grated orange rind.

4 Tip the fruit into the base of a lightly oiled 1.5 litre/2½ pint/ 6¼ cups ring mould. Spoon in the rice, smoothing it down firmly, then chill.

5 Run a knife around the edge of the mould then carefully turn out the rice ring onto a serving plate.

Yellow Rice Pudding

INGREDIENTS

Serves 6–8

225g/8oz/generous 1 cup short grain
   pudding rice
1.5 litres/2½ pints/6¼ cups water
350g/12oz/1½ cups caster sugar
2–3 saffron strands, dissolved in 15ml/
   1tbsp boiling water
60ml/4 tbsp rose water
2.5ml/½ tsp ground cardamom seeds
50g/2oz/¼ cup chopped
   blanched almonds
25g/1oz/2 tbsp butter
25g/1oz/¼ cup chopped pistachios
5ml/1 tsp ground cinnamon

1 Preheat the oven to 150°C/300°F/
Gas 2. Place the rice and water in a
large pan, bring to the boil and simmer
until the rice is soft and swollen.

2 Pour 250ml/8fl oz/1 cup water
into another saucepan, add the
sugar and simmer for 10 minutes. Add
the saffron, rose water, cardamom and
half the almonds. Stir well.

3 Pour the syrup over the rice, add
the butter and stir well.

4 Pour the rice mixture into an
ovenproof dish, cover with a lid or
with a sheet of foil and bake in the
oven for 30 minutes.

5 Remove the pudding from the
oven and decorate with the
remaining almonds and the pistachios.
Dust with cinnamon and then serve
warm or chill before serving.

Caramel Rice Pudding

This rice pudding is delicious served with crunchy fresh fruit.

INGREDIENTS

Serves 4

50g/2oz/4 tbsp short grain
   pudding rice
75ml/5 tbsp demerara sugar
pinch of salt
400g/14oz can evaporated milk
   made up to 600ml/1 pint/2½ cups
   with water
knob of butter
1 small fresh pineapple
2 crisp eating apples
10ml/2 tsp lemon juice

1 Preheat the oven to 150°C/300°F/
Gas 2. Put the rice in a sieve and
wash thoroughly under cold water.
Drain well and put into a lightly
greased soufflé dish.

2 Add 30ml/2 tbsp sugar and the salt
to the dish. Pour on the diluted
evaporated milk and stir gently.

3 Dot the surface of the rice with
butter and bake for 2 hours, then
leave to cool for 30 minutes.

4 Meanwhile, peel, core and slice the
pineapple and apples and then cut
the pineapple into chunks. Toss the
fruit in lemon juice and set aside.

5 Preheat the grill and sprinkle the
remaining sugar over the rice. Grill
for 5 minutes or until the sugar has
caramelized. Leave the rice to stand for
5 minutes to allow the caramel to
harden, then serve with the fresh fruit.

Spiced Rice Pudding

Both Muslim and Hindu
communities prepare this
pudding, which is traditionally
served at mosques and temples.

INGREDIENTS

Serves 4–6

15ml/1 tbsp ghee or melted
   unsalted butter
5cm/2in piece cinnamon stick
225g/8oz/1 cup soft brown sugar
115g/4oz/½ cup ground rice
1.2 litres/2 pints/5 cups milk
5ml/1 tsp ground cardamom seeds
50g/2oz/scant ½ cup sultanas
25g/1oz/¼ cup slivered almonds
2.5ml/½ tsp grated nutmeg, to serve

1 In a heavy pan, heat the ghee or
butter and fry the cinnamon and
sugar. Keep frying until the sugar
begins to caramelize. Reduce the heat
immediately when this happens.

2 Add the rice and half of the milk.
Bring to the boil, stirring
constantly to avoid the milk boiling
over. Reduce the heat and simmer until
the rice is cooked, stirring regularly.

3 Add the remaining milk,
cardamom, sultanas and almonds
and leave to simmer, but keep stirring
to prevent the rice from sticking to the
base of the pan. When the mixture has
thickened, serve hot or cold, sprinkled
with the grated nutmeg.

Black Glutinous Rice Pudding

This unusual rice pudding uses bruised fresh root ginger and is quite delicious. Serve in small bowls, with a little coconut cream poured over.

INGREDIENTS

Serves 6

115g/4oz/generous ½ cup black
   glutinous rice
475ml/16fl oz/2 cups water
1cm/½ in fresh root ginger, peeled
   and bruised
50g/2oz/¼ cup dark brown sugar
50g/2oz/¼ cup caster sugar
300ml/½ pint/1¼ cups coconut milk
   or cream, to serve

1 Put the rice in a sieve and rinse well under cold running water. Drain and put in a large pan with the water. Bring to the boil and stir once to prevent the rice sticking to the pan. Cover and cook for about 30 minutes.

2 Add the ginger and both the brown and caster sugars. Cook for a further 15 minutes, adding a little more water if necessary, until the rice is thoroughly cooked and porridge-like.

3 Remove the ginger from the rice mixture and serve the pudding warm, in bowls, topped with coconut milk or cream.

— COOK'S TIP —

For a fresh coconut flavour, choose tetra-packs of coconut cream instead of canned coconut milk. Alternatively, blend a little creamed coconut block with hot water until thick and creamy then allow to cool before serving.

Souffléed Rice Pudding

Using skimmed milk to make this pudding is a healthy option, but you could use whole milk if you prefer.

INGREDIENTS

Serves 4

65g/2½ oz/generous ¼ cup short grain pudding rice
45ml/3 tbsp clear honey
750ml/1¼ pints/3 cups skimmed milk
1 vanilla pod or 2.5ml/½ tsp vanilla essence
2 egg whites
5ml/1 tsp freshly grated nutmeg

1 Place the rice, honey and milk in a heavy or non-stick saucepan, and bring the milk to the boil, being careful it does not boil over. Add the vanilla pod, if using.

2 Reduce the heat and cover the pan. Leave to simmer gently for about 1-1¼ hours, stirring occasionally to prevent sticking, until most of the liquid has been absorbed.

3 Remove the vanilla pod or, if using vanilla essence, add this to the rice mixture now. Preheat the oven to 220°C/425°F/Gas 7.

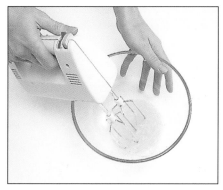

4 Place the egg whites in a large clean, dry bowl and whisk them until they hold in soft peaks.

5 Using either a large metal spoon or a spatula, carefully fold the egg whites evenly into the rice and milk mixture. Tip into a 1 litre/1¾ pints/ 4 cups ovenproof dish.

6 Sprinkle with grated nutmeg and bake for about 15-20 minutes, until the pudding is well risen and golden brown. Serve hot.

Index